Getting the Full Picture on Public Officials

Stolen Asset Recovery (StAR) Series

StAR—the Stolen Asset Recovery Initiative—is a partnership between the World Bank Group and the United Nations Office on Drugs and Crime (UNODC) that supports international efforts to end safe havens for corrupt funds. StAR works with developing countries and financial centers to prevent the laundering of the proceeds of corruption and to facilitate more systematic and timely return of stolen assets.

The Stolen Asset Recovery (StAR) Series supports the efforts of StAR and UNODC by providing practitioners with knowledge and policy tools that consolidate international good practice and wide-ranging practical experience on cutting edge issues related to anti-corruption and asset recovery efforts. For more information, visit www.worldbank.org/star.

Titles in the Stolen Asset Recovery (StAR) Series

Stolen Asset Recovery: A Good Practices Guide for Non-Conviction Based Asset Forfeiture (2009) by Theodore S. Greenberg, Linda M. Samuel, Wingate Grant, and Larissa Gray

Politically Exposed Persons: Preventive Measures for the Banking Sector (2010) by Theodore S. Greenberg, Larissa Gray, Delphine Schantz, Carolin Gardner, and Michael Latham

Asset Recovery Handbook: A Guide for Practitioners (2011) by Jean-Pierre Brun, Larissa Gray, Clive Scott, and Kevin Stephenson

Barriers to Asset Recovery: An Analysis of the Key Barriers and Recommendations for Action (2011) by Kevin Stephenson, Larissa Gray, and Ric Power

The Puppet Masters: How the Corrupt Use Legal Structures to Hide Stolen Assets and What to Do About It (2011) by Emile van der Does de Willebois, J. C. Sharman, Robert Harrison, Ji Won Park, and Emily Halter

Public Office, Private Interests: Accountability through Income and Asset Disclosure (2012)

On the Take: Criminalizing Illicit Enrichment to Fight Corruption (2012) by Lindy Muzila, Michelle Morales, Marianne Mathias, and Tammar Berger

Left Out of the Bargain: Settlements in Foreign Bribery Cases and Implications for Asset Recovery (2014) by Jacinta Anyango Oduor, Francisca M. U. Fernando, Agustin Flah, Dorothee Gottwald, Jeanne M. Hauch, Marianne Mathias, Ji Won Park, and Oliver Stolpe

Public Wrongs, Private Actions: Civil Lawsuits to Recover Stolen Assets (2015) by Jean-Pierre Brun, Pascale Helene Dubois, Emile van der Does de Willebois, Jeanne Hauch, Sarah Jaïs, Yannis Mekki, Anastasia Sotiropoulou, Katherine Rose Sylvester, and Mahesh Uttamchandani

Getting the Full Picture on Public Officials: A How-to Guide for Effective Financial Disclosure (2017) by Ivana M. Rossi, Laura Pop, and Tammar Berger

All books in the StAR Series are available for free at https://openknowledge.worldbank.org/handle/10986/2172.

Getting the Full Picture on Public Officials

A How-to Guide for Effective Financial Disclosure

Ivana M. Rossi
Laura Pop
Tammar Berger

Stolen Asset Recovery Initiative

The World Bank • UNODC

Contents

Tables

Foreword

In a series of articles titled "Towers of Secrecy," the *New York Times* in 2015 revealed the opaque way in which much high-value U.S. real estate is owned by famous and politically connected persons from around the world. The anticorruption organization Transparency International conducted a similar exercise in the United Kingdom, showing how (among others) apartments in the exclusive London boroughs of Kensington and Chelsea were owned by shell companies. More recently, information leaked from the Bahamas and Panama law firm Mossack Fonseca revealed that many of the world's famous and politically powerful individuals own assets in such convoluted ways that their control over those assets is all but invisible to the outside world. Time then, to take a good look at some of the tools that could help shed light on the assets of the powerful. Time for a book on financial disclosure—the rules on what those in power should declare, to whom and how, about the assets they own and interests they hold.

By now, 161 countries around the world have introduced financial disclosure systems. Since their initial introduction in the United States following the Watergate affair, they have become commonplace around the world. But, although the rules are on the books, many practitioners are still struggling with the intricacies of the rules and how to implement them in the socioeconomic, historical, and legal contexts of their own countries. Little guidance is available to assist them. This book aims to fill that void and provide practitioners with practical scenarios to consider before deciding on a particular course of action.

This book contains short chapters that elaborate each topic and provide clear guidance on the issues that policy makers and those involved in the implementation of financial disclosure obligations will need to take into account before making a decision. How do you decide *who* should file? Everyone in the civil service? Only ministers? And what about their spouses, children, or extended family? And how often? Online or in hard copy? And what exactly? Everything they own directly—or also those apartments they own indirectly? This is the sort of practical guidance that this book aims to provide.

At the World Bank, we consider information on the interests and assets of those who wield public power to be a vital element of good governance and anticorruption. Financial disclosure systems are a vital component of transparency. The only societies that provide the necessary checks to power that are needed to underpin growth and development are those that ask their leaders to provide complete information on what they have and where their interests lie, and that are able to hold leaders to account in the event of deficiencies or omissions. Moreover, financial information is very useful for those conducting corruption and money-laundering investigations. We hope that the practitioners who use this book will find it to be a useful tool in guiding their decision making, and, ultimately, to help their countries build more effective systems.

Gloria Grandolini
Senior Director, Finance and Markets Global Practice
World Bank Group

Acknowledgments

This Guide was written by a Stolen Asset Recovery Initiative (StAR) and World Bank Group (WBG) team comprising Ivana M. Rossi, Laura Pop, and Tammar Berger, under the guidance of Jean Pesme (former StAR Coordinator and Practice Manager, Financial Market Integrity, WBG). This Guide also draws on financial disclosure systems data gathered throughout the years by a WBG team, most recently comprising Catherine Greene, Tanya Blackburn, and Gaukhar Larson, and with earlier contributions from Simeon Djankov, Elena Gasol-Ramos, Francesco Clementucci, Larisa Smirnova, Lina Sawaqed, Teymour Abdel-Aziz, Hania Dawood, Doina Cebotari, Joyce Ibrahim, and Stephanie Musialski.

The team gratefully acknowledges the expert guidance and advice of peer reviewers Oliver Stolpe (Chief, Conference Support Section, Corruption and Economic Crime Branch Division for Treaty Affairs, United Nations Office on Drugs and Crime [UNODC]), Silviu Popa (Deputy Director, National Integrity Agency of Romania), Marko Klasnja (Assistant Professor, School of Foreign Service and Government Department, Georgetown University), Jana Kunikova (Senior Public Sector Specialist, Governance Global Practice, WBG), and Alexandra Habershon (Program Coordinator, Integrity Vice Presidency, WBG).

Emile Van der Does de Willebois (StAR/WBG), Lisa Bostwick (StAR/WBG), Nigel Bartlett (StAR/WBG), Stuart Yikona (WBG), Elsa Gopala Krishnan (StAR/UNODC), and Emily Adeleke (WBG) have also generously contributed their advice and experience to this Guide. Ladan Cherenegar and Liudmila Uvarova provided support at different stages of the project.

The team wishes to thank Gloria Grandolini (Senior Director, Finance and Markets Global Practice, WBG), Alfonso Garcia Mora (Director, Finance and Markets Global Practice), and our current Practice Manager, Yira Mascaró (Financial Market Integrity/StAR, WBG) for their support in the completion of this project.

Finally, the team would like to acknowledge all the hard-working practitioners in the financial disclosure field who have interacted and worked with the team throughout the years and who have invaluably contributed to this Guide.

About the Authors

Ivana M. Rossi is a Senior Financial Sector Specialist with the World Bank's Financial Market Integrity/StAR Initiative team. She has led the work on financial disclosure by public officials since 2009, providing tailored technical assistance to countries, enhancing knowledge-sharing at the regional and global levels, developing research, and contributing to international policy debates on disclosure, such as the G-20 Anti-Corruption Working Group and Open Government Partnership. Her work promotes innovation and synergies with the anti-money-laundering and asset recovery fields. She has authored "Using Asset Disclosure for Identifying Politically Exposed Persons" (World Bank) and other analytical work, such as the Financial Disclosure Law Library, articles, and blogs. Before joining the World Bank in 2006, she worked in different transparency and public sector reform initiatives in international organizations, as well as in the civil society sector in Argentina.

Laura Pop is a Senior Financial Sector Specialist with the World Bank's Financial Market Integrity/StAR Initiative team. Since joining the World Bank in 2009, she has delivered advisory services on multiple areas of asset declaration (enhancing the legal framework; transitioning from paper to electronic filing; increasing the effectiveness of verification; operationalizing the concept of beneficial ownership in declarations; and establishing interagency cooperation, in particular with anti-money-laundering institutions) to more than 20 countries across all regions. She coauthored "Using Asset Disclosure for Identifying Politically Exposed Persons" (World Bank). She designed and worked on the content of the Financial Disclosure Law Library, the first collection of laws and regulations on disclosure from 176 jurisdictions. She also works on asset recovery, anti-money-laundering, and financial inclusion/integrity programs. She holds a BA from Princeton University and an MA from Harvard University.

Tammar Berger is a consultant with the StAR Initiative, where she focuses on anti-corruption and asset recovery efforts. She has also worked with the World Bank's Governance and Public Sector Management Unit on transparency and accountability mechanisms. She holds a JD from Georgetown University Law Center and an MA in international relations from Johns Hopkins University's Paul H. Nitze School of Advanced International Studies.

Abbreviations

AML/CFT	anti-money-laundering and combating the financing of terrorism
APEC	Asia-Pacific Economic Cooperation
AUCC	African Union Convention against Corruption
FATF	Financial Action Task Force
FIU	financial intelligence unit
G-20	Group of Twenty
HR	human resources
IACAC	Inter-American Convention against Corruption
M&E	monitoring and evaluation
ML/TF	money-laundering and terrorism financing
OECD	Organisation for Economic Co-operation and Development
PEP	politically exposed person
StAR	Stolen Asset Recovery Initiative (World Bank and UNODC)
UNCAC	United Nations Convention against Corruption
UNODC	United Nations Office on Drugs and Crime

Glossary

Financial disclosure: A mechanism by which a public official must periodically submit information about his or her income, assets, liabilities, and/or interests. Also referred to as *asset disclosure, income and asset declarations, wealth reporting,* and *interest declarations.*

Financial disclosure agency: A government entity in charge of managing the financial disclosure system. Disclosure management can be centralized in a single agency or decentralized. Depending on the system's design and its objectives, the agency can be autonomous or act under the scope of one of the three branches of power.

Beneficial owner: "The natural person who ultimately owns or controls the corporate vehicle or benefits from its assets, the person on whose behalf a transaction is being conducted, or both. Beneficial owners also include those persons who exercise ultimate effective control over a legal person or arrangement" (FATF 2012).

Compliance: The fulfillment by public officials of their disclosure obligations established by law.

Conflict of interest: A situation that has the potential to undermine a public official's impartiality because of a personal interest that is opposed to the public interest.

FATF Recommendations: The International Standards on Combating Money Laundering and the Financing of Terrorism and Proliferation adopted by the Financial Action Task Force in February 2012 and updated in 2013 and 2014. The standards establish a comprehensive framework of measures for signatory countries to implement in order to combat money laundering, terrorist financing, and financing of proliferation of weapons of mass destruction.

Financial intelligence unit: "A central, national agency responsible for receiving (and as permitted, requesting), analyzing, and disseminating to the competent authorities, disclosures of financial information (i) concerning suspected proceeds of crime and potential financing of terrorism, or (ii) required by national legislation or regulation, in order to combat money laundering and terrorism financing."[1]

Illicit enrichment: "A significant increase in the assets of a public official that he or she cannot reasonably explain in relation to his or her lawful income" (UN 2004, article 20).

List of filers: Document created by a financial disclosure agency that identifies the positions required to declare assets and that is populated with the names of officials occupying those positions.

Mutual legal assistance: "The process by which jurisdictions seek and provide assistance in gathering information, intelligence, and evidence for investigations; in implementing provisional measures; and in enforcing foreign orders and judgments" (Brun and others 2011, 251).

Open source information: Data that can be obtained from publicly available resources.

Politically exposed person: "Individuals who are, or have been, entrusted with prominent public functions, their family members, and close associates" (FATF 2012).

Submission: The process through which the public official presents to the financial disclosure agency all the information requested. It includes the filing of financial disclosure forms and also entails the preliminary check of the information received, the data management or transfer, and the communication with filers.

Verification: The process of checking and analyzing the information disclosed. It may entail different types of actions such as monitoring, reviewing, inspecting, and auditing. Depending on the system's design, verification may be a single-step process (such as screening for internal consistencies) or a multiple-step one (that may include checking for internal consistency, analyzing variations across years, and even comparing the declared data with outside sources of information).

Note

1. Definition adopted at the plenary meeting of the Egmont Group in Rome, Italy, in November 1996, and amended at the Egmont plenary meeting in Guernsey, United Kingdom, in June 2004.

References

Brun, J.-P., L. Gray, C. Scott, and K. M. Stephenson. 2011. *Asset Recovery Handbook: A Guide for Practitioners*. Washington, DC: World Bank.

FATF (Financial Action Task Force). 2012. *International Standards on Combating Money Laundering and the Financing of Terrorism and Proliferation*. Paris: FATF. http://www.fatf -gafi.org/media/fatf/documents/recommendations/pdfs/FATF_Recommendations.pdf.

UN (United Nations). 2004. *United Nations Convention against Corruption*. 2004. New York: UN. https://www.unodc.org/documents/treaties/UNCAC/Publications /Convention/08-50026_E.pdf.

Introduction

At the time of his death in 2012, Bingu wa Mutharika, former president of Malawi, had allegedly amassed US$120 million in wealth. Public records indicate that, when Mutharika took office in 2004, he declared personal wealth amounting to US$35,000 (Mtika 2015). Jérôme Cahuzac, former budget minister of France, admitted to lying not only to the tax authority but also in his financial disclosure about bank accounts held in Switzerland and Singapore, where he hid away at least €600,000 (Bamat and Oberti 2013; Reuters 2013). Former President of Argentina Cristina Fernández de Kirchner and her late husband, former President Néstor Kirchner, held power for 12 years combined; according to their financial disclosures, their wealth went from Arg$7 million to Arg$64 million in that period (Ruiz and Jastreblansky 2015).

It takes only a quick Internet search to find stories like this across the world. Allegations differ; however, the common thread is the filing of financial disclosures by public officials. *Financial disclosure, asset disclosure, income and asset declarations, wealth reporting*, and *interest declarations*—despite the variations in name,[1] all of these mechanisms are bound by a common and simple principle: a public official must periodically submit information about his or her income, assets, liabilities, and interests.

Incorporated into several international conventions, including the United Nations Convention against Corruption, financial disclosure systems are widespread across regions and are recognized as a key tool in the fight against corruption and in promoting transparency.

Much has been written on this topic,[2] so why a new publication? Because there is much more to be said about disclosure and its practical implementation. We believe disclosure mechanisms have been underestimated and underutilized. An effective disclosure system can play a central role in promoting transparency, accountability, integrity, and ethical behavior in the public sector, while also acting as a fundamental link in the broader anticorruption chain. For example, consider the following:

- When a public official feels confident enough to show to the world that his or her assets and interests have been legally earned and pose no risk of conflicts of interest, the system promotes *a culture of integrity* and *builds trust in the public sector.*
- When a disclosure form becomes a way to provide guidance to public officials on how to avoid conflicts of interest, the disclosure system *encourages ethical behavior.*
- When a public official knows that disclosures are routinely screened and that corrupt activity might be exposed, the system can deter misbehavior and enhance corruption prevention.

- When the media denounces a public official for an inaccurate disclosure, the system *promotes accountability*. And when authorities formally look into such denouncements, disclosures become a *source of information for an investigation* and, potentially, *evidence*.
- When a disclosure is used to identify politically exposed persons or to provide valuable *information for other offenses*, it can *support anti-money-laundering or asset recovery efforts*, which extend far beyond the disclosure's original purpose.

As means to these various ends, disclosures deserve greater attention. A closer look is also timely because many countries have recently stepped up the implementation of disclosure regimes, and there are many new experiences to take stock of. With the integration of new technologies and enhancements in coordination with other areas, the potential for using disclosures to fight corruption is growing. This Guide aims to capture and contribute to this momentum, while also helping countries make full use of this tool. The Guide aims to assist both practitioners in countries embarking on a brand new financial disclosure system, as well as practitioners in countries with existing systems seeking to improve or enhance effectiveness. Moreover, this Guide might be useful for civil society and those involved in academic research.

The key to achieving the full potential of a simple declaration is building an *effective* disclosure system. First, let's unpack the term *financial disclosure system*. This refers to the entire process of disclosing assets and interests, from the blank form to submission, verification, and sanctioning. Each step is a necessary and integral part of an effective system. So, what makes a disclosure system effective? This is the question that this Guide aims to answer. But beware, there might not be a single answer.

In answering this question we aim to achieve two objectives. The first is to support the policy and operational decisions of practitioners and to contribute to *greater effectiveness* in their work. The second is to inform the global dialogue on *good practices and principles* on disclosure that have developed in recent years.[3]

To analyze the effectiveness of disclosure systems, we take two complementary approaches, the descriptive and the analytical. The descriptive approach looks at the disclosure systems already in place. This entails looking at how countries have designed and implemented their current systems. In order to do so, we gathered two sets of data (see box I.2.) The first covers the disclosure provisions of 176 countries, with an emphasis on the foundational legal requirements of each system. The second assesses the most common practices in 52 countries, with a focus on implementation.[4] In other words, one data set looks at issues by law, while the other looks at practice[5] (see box I.2).

The second approach analyzes the lessons learned from the Stolen Asset Recovery Initiative's (StAR) work in providing technical assistance to countries around the world to strengthen their disclosure systems (see box I.1). We identified the key challenges that were consistent across all regions, from Asia to the Americas and from Europe to Africa. Although capacity, resources, objectives, priorities, and legal and political

BOX I.1   Who Are We?

The Stolen Asset Recovery Initiative (StAR) is a partnership between the World Bank Group and the United Nations Office on Drugs and Crime that supports international efforts to eliminate safe havens for corrupt funds. StAR works with developing countries and financial centers to prevent the laundering of the proceeds of corruption and to facilitate more systematic and timely return of stolen assets. StAR works with the Financial Market Integrity (FMI) team of the World Bank Group on this topic. FMI has been working on financial disclosure since 2007, analyzing disclosure for public officials across the world and producing detailed data for 176 countries. Together we provide technical assistance to countries with both emerging and established financial disclosure systems, and have helped more than 30 countries to date. We develop and deliver outreach and knowledge products, with a focus on innovation and identifying synergies with anti-money-laundering and asset recovery, organizing international events in five regions, and informing international dialogue on this topic, including with the G-20 Anti-Corruption Working Group and Open Government Partnership. For more information on our work, please refer to http://star.worldbank.org/star/ and http://www.worldbank.org/en/topic/financialmarketintegrity/brief/financial-disclosure.

BOX I.2   A Little Bit More on Our Data

This Guide builds on the data that the World Bank has been collecting since 2007 on the legislation and functioning of disclosure systems across the world. The data collected for 176 jurisdictions focus on the legal framework underpinning disclosure systems and the main features of the systems (for example, officials subject to disclosure, content of the disclosure form, agency responsible for monitoring content of disclosures, sanctions for nonsubmission, submission of inaccurate information, and so on). According to our research, of the 176 countries in the sample, 161 have a disclosure system.

These data are complemented by a smaller sample, covering 52 countries, focusing on the practices of disclosure agencies. The main topics covered by the research are procedures for the collection of financial disclosures, the use of technology for submission and monitoring of disclosures, access to disclosed information by the public and by public sector entities, and approaches to monitoring the content of disclosures.

The countries for the smaller sample were selected from those jurisdictions that, according to the research, have more established disclosure systems. Furthermore, we focused on countries whose experiences provide data across several implementation issues, while maintaining regional balance. Finally, we selected disclosure systems whose experiences have the potential to provide valuable insights for the identification of trends and innovation in the implementation of financial disclosure.

For more on our data collection methodology as well as a full list of countries covered in our sample, please see appendix A.

frameworks differ greatly, we have identified consistent lessons and good practices in the implementation of effective financial disclosure systems.

As with every kind of system, the effectiveness of financial disclosure depends on each of its parts. They are all interdependent and fundamental to the success of the whole. For this reason, this Guide is divided into chapters, each covering a key aspect of financial disclosure systems. The Guide does not provide standard answers or unique best practices. However, all systems face common challenges and must address similar fundamental questions. Each chapter thus focuses on a fundamental point that must be addressed for effective implementation of a disclosure system.

Even though the Guide shares information on existing legal systems, it does not concentrate on the drafting of legislation. Most countries already have legislation on disclosure. Introducing amendments or new legislation can be a difficult and lengthy task, and in certain cases, politically infeasible. We believe that a stronger understanding of what is entailed in effective implementation will provide valuable input for everyday work and for later adoption of more informed provisions. Learning from others' experiences will help readers avoid embedding common mistakes into their systems. Our aim is that, when the time comes, the lessons learned from the implementation of disclosure systems will contribute to the drafting of stronger laws.

The first chapter focuses on *why* countries need financial disclosure systems and the objectives commonly pursued. The second chapter addresses *who* should file a disclosure and how often. The third chapter delves into *what* public officials should declare. The fourth chapter focuses on *how, where, and by which means* disclosures should be submitted. The fifth chapter looks into *how to check information* submitted in disclosures. The sixth chapter covers *public access* to information in the disclosures as well as *information-sharing*. The final chapter describes the types of *sanctions* associated with disclosure and how financial disclosures can support the investigation and prosecution of corruption cases. Please keep in mind that each chapter can be read in sequence or independently.

Reading this Guide, one may note that some important topics are not comprehensively addressed. Thus, this Guide should be read with several caveats in mind. The first is that of political will. Some level of political will is needed in the implementation of every single step of the financial disclosure system. Political will is an elusive element that is difficult both to attain and to quantify. That said, it is possible to work within the limitations set by varying levels of political will. Recognizing that yes, one may operate in an imperfect system, but something can still be done.

Another caveat that needs emphasis is the need to manage expectations. Although there is much discussion in the Guide about the potential of disclosure systems to have a substantial impact, it is important to note that (a) there are still limited data on the magnitude of the impact of disclosures on combating corruption and increasing accountability, and (b) the impact of disclosures will be constrained by the context in which a system operates. Implementing a disclosure system in a country where there is limited political will, corruption is widespread, tax systems are dysfunctional, or law enforcement is weak will not automatically fix these issues. It will not be the silver bullet. However, a well-designed and operational system of financial disclosure can serve as a step in the right direction and can be an important element in the overall anticorruption and integrity system of a country.

A third caveat relates to the objectives of the disclosure system. Although this Guide discusses both systems that are geared towards detecting illicit wealth and systems that seek to identify, manage, and sanction conflicts of interest, there is more emphasis on the former. This does not mean that conflicts of interest are any less important, but is simply a reflection of our experience. We have found that in many countries that do not belong to the Organisation for Economic Co-operation and Development (OECD), conflict of interest (COI) legislation or regulation is either limited or absent. If such laws do exist, more often than not, implementation is just beginning or lagging. This is why, for many aspects of COI systems outside OECD countries, it is too early to identify trends and to discuss lessons learned. As this is an area in which we are seeing increasing interest, we expect to be able to provide more comprehensive coverage of COI practices in a future publication.

Also absent from this Guide is a thorough discussion of the role of monitoring and evaluation in disclosure systems. This is due to the fact that there is limited experience available on this topic. Most disclosure institutions are still focusing on building the foundational elements of the system and on implementing core operational functions. However, there are some emerging good practices in this area, such as tracking the follow-up of financial disclosure findings and the number and names of officials who disclose and those who fail to declare. Although we do not devote a chapter or section to this topic, we will note here that monitoring and evaluation (M&E) can and should be included when implementing an effective financial disclosure system, as it provides the necessary feedback to inform policy changes. Additionally, it may provide the empirical evidence on what makes a disclosure system effective, which is still lacking on a global level. As such, including M&E in the design of disclosure systems can not only go a long a way in increasing the effectiveness of the disclosure system itself, but can also serve to bolster the role disclosure takes in combating corruption and in promoting transparency and accountability.

One final caveat for this Guide is the underlying nexus of financial disclosure, asset recovery, and the global fight against corruption. The potential role for financial disclosure systems in this larger context is, though as yet largely untapped, significant. It is our hope that this Guide will help foster stronger disclosure systems, which may, in turn, pave the way for this potential to be realized.

Notes

1. Please note that these are used as synonyms across this Guide.
2. See, for example, Djankov and others (2010), OECD (2011), and StAR (2012).
3. For more on this, please see chapter 1 of this Guide.

4. For more on this data set, please refer to appendix A.
5. Please note that the data sets resulting from our data collection exercises are not public, as our aim is to provide *aggregate* information on financial disclosure. However, all of the laws consulted during our research are available at www .worldbank.org/fpd/financialdisclosure/lawlibrary.

References

Bamat, J., and C. Oberti. 2013. "French Politicians Rush to Reveal Their Assets." *France 24*, April 9. http://www.france24.com/en/20130409-france-politicians -assets-disclosure-tax-fraud-scandal-hollande-socialist.

Brun, J.-P., L. Gray, C. Scott, and K. M. Stephenson. 2011. *Asset Recovery Handbook: A Guide for Practitioners*. Washington, DC: World Bank.

Djankov, S., R. La Porta, F. Lopez-de-Silanes, and A. Shleifer. 2010. "Disclosure By Politicians." *American Economic Journal: Applied Economics* 2 (April): 179–209.

FATF (Financial Action Task Force). 2012. *International Standards on Combating Money Laundering and the Financing of Terrorism and Proliferation*. Paris: FATF. http://www.fatf-gafi.org/media/fatf/documents/recommendations/pdfs/FATF _Recommendations.pdf.

Mtika, C. 2015. "Malawi President's Assets Open for Inspection." *African Independent*, December 16. http://www.africanindy.com/business/malawi-presidents-assets-open -for-inspection-1465353.

OECD (Organisation for Economic Co-operation and Development). 2011. *Asset Declarations for Public Officials: A Tool to Prevent Corruption*. Paris: OECD.

Reuters. 2013. "France to Publish Ministers' Assets As Scandal Deepens." *Chicago Tribune*, April 8. http://articles.chicagotribune.com/2013-04-08/news/sns-rt-us -france-ministerbre9370kq-20130408_1_bank-account-jerome-cahuzac-president -francois-hollande.

Ruiz, I., and M. Jastreblanksy. 2015. "El crecimiento de la fortuna de los Kirchner: de 7 a 100 millones." *La Nacion*, March 8. http://www.lanacion.com.ar/1852228-el -crecimiento-de-la-fortuna-de-los-kirchner-de-7-a-100-millones.

StAR (Stolen Asset Recovery Initiative). 2012. *Public Office, Private Interests: Accountability through Income and Asset Disclosure*. Washington, DC: World Bank.

UN (United Nations). 2004. *United Nations Convention against Corruption*. New York: UN. https://www.unodc.org/documents/treaties/UNCAC/Publications/Convention /08-50026_E.pdf.

1. Why Do Countries Embark on Financial Disclosure?

When we asked a former public official of a Latin American country why that country had decided to create a financial disclosure system before the turn of the century, the answer was clear: to comply with the Inter-American Convention against Corruption of 1996. A scandal involving a former French budget minister and his hidden Swiss bank accounts triggered a comprehensive amendment of France's transparency laws in 2013. In 2014 in Ukraine, the restructuring of the country's anticorruption framework was in direct response to the high-level corruption of the Yanukovych regime. In Romania, an overhaul of the disclosure system was necessary to demonstrate commitment to the fight against corruption and to overcome its greatest obstacle to the country's accession to the European Union.

As these examples illustrate, countries have different motivations for establishing or strengthening financial disclosure systems: prime ones (a) help detect and prevent corrupt behavior, perhaps in response to scandals involving high-level public officials, and (b) bolster public confidence in the integrity of a government with a questionable history. A financial disclosure system can also aim to build a climate of integrity in public service, prevent abuse of power under a new political administration, or simply boost compliance with international obligations or eligibility to participate in certain international fora.

Awareness of the importance of financial disclosure is growing, but what is driving this interest? Why are international bodies such as the Group of 20 (G-20) raising the bar in the implementation of these systems? What is motivating an increasing number of governments to implement disclosure practices? Countries have different reasons for developing financial disclosure systems, but, though there is limited evidence to date of the impact of an effective system, the links to larger developmental goals, such as fostering integrity in public service and strengthening the fight against corruption, are both evident and important.

Regardless of the rationale for implementing or strengthening a financial disclosure system, it is important to keep in mind that this opens the possibility of building a powerful tool. But not all systems are built alike; rather, the diversity of financial disclosure systems reflects their multiple uses and objectives. The purpose of this chapter is to look more closely at these different approaches.

Global and Regional Trends Observed in the Adoption of Disclosure Systems

Financial disclosure frameworks are not new. They began to appear in the 1950s and started to slowly gain momentum in the 1970s in the wake of the Watergate corruption scandal in the United States.[1] As concerns about potential conflicts of interest (COI) grew, more countries began enacting laws that require officials to disclose their financial information, including information related to assets, income, and liabilities. After years of modest growth, the adoption of financial disclosure laws has spiked globally in the past three decades (figure 1.1). The United Nations Convention against Corruption (UNCAC) invigorated efforts in 2003 with the inclusion of financial disclosure as part of its mechanisms to enhance transparency,[2] as did other regional and international instruments designed to combat the global challenges of corruption.[3]

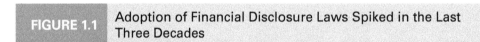

FIGURE 1.1 Adoption of Financial Disclosure Laws Spiked in the Last Three Decades

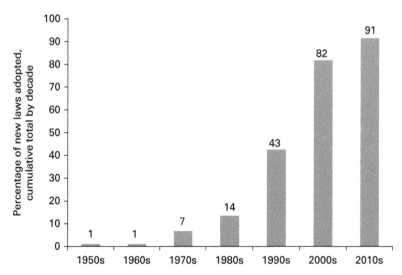

Note: Approximate percentages based on the analysis of 158 disclosure jurisdictions.

Although the growth of financial disclosure systems has been global and widespread, some regions are moving faster than others. Growth trends are often dictated by the strength of domestic commitment to prioritizing anticorruption measures (including financial disclosure systems), the level of disclosure in neighboring countries, and the availability of regional instruments or guidelines. For example, 93 percent of countries in Latin America and the Caribbean have financial disclosure legislation in place; that share drops to 73 percent in Asia and to 61 percent in the Middle East and North Africa (figure 1.2.)

FIGURE 1.2 **Financial Disclosure Laws Are More Widespread in Some Regions**

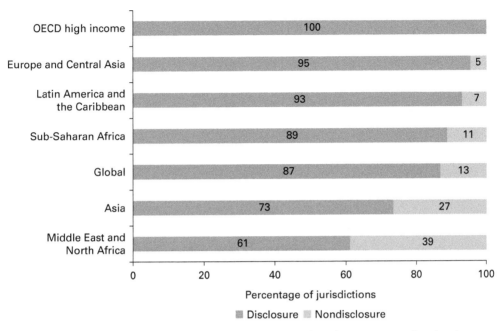

Note: OECD = Organisation for Economic Co-operation and Development. Approximate percentages based on the analysis of 176 jurisdictions.

The adoption and implementation of financial disclosure systems is still growing, with a handful of countries adding or reforming financial disclosure laws in the past year alone.[4] Despite growth both in the number of countries with disclosure laws and in the role that disclosure plays in international efforts to combat corruption, it is important to note that financial disclosure provisions have not always translated into effective systems. Implementation of financial disclosure laws is often lagging, ineffectual, or at times nonexistent, leaving a large gap between systems "in law" and "in practice." To close this gap, the implementation of financial disclosure laws should always take the system's overall objective as a point of departure.

> It is important to note that financial disclosure provisions have not always translated into effective systems.

What Are the Objectives of a Disclosure System?

The underlying objective for many financial disclosure systems is to support the creation of a culture of integrity, as set out by the UNCAC:

> As a general principle, public bodies … need to create a climate where the public service provision is transparent and impartial, where it is known that the offering and acceptance

of gifts and hospitality is not encouraged, and where personal or other interests should not appear to influence official actions and decisions. (UNODC 2009, 25)[5]

The immediate objectives of financial disclosure are specific to each country; thus, each system is designed differently. Differences are noticeable in all areas, from who is mandated to declare, to the type of information requested, the use of that information, and even the agency in charge of managing the system.

Illicit Wealth Focus

Countries that aim to prevent and investigate or prosecute corruption focus on detecting illicit wealth. To that end, they seek to capture information and monitor the wealth of public officials across time in an effort to detect unusual or unexplained assets or income. Disclosure forms typically gather details about movable and immovable assets, income, stocks and securities, and liabilities. These forms focus on values to allow for financial analysis across time. In these countries, the agency in charge of managing the system (the financial disclosure agency) tends to be autonomous, with a mandate linked to anticorruption or auditing, and devotes resources to monitoring disclosure forms for irregularities.

Countries experiencing widespread corruption are all too familiar with the difficulty of detecting and prosecuting corruption crimes such as bribery and embezzlement. By implementing a disclosure system that is designed to detect illicit enrichment, a country can monitor and flag significant and *prima facie* inexplicable changes in public officials' wealth. Such a system can allow for the investigation and conviction of corrupt officials and the recovery of stolen assets.

Conflict of Interest Focus

A country seeking to prevent misuse of public office requires a system designed to inform and guide public officials on conflicts of interest. Such systems are indeed designed to identify potential conflicts of interest rather than to detect improper conduct. Disclosure systems focused on conflicts of interest typically request the following information: positions held outside of office, sources of income, gifts, and names of companies in which the official has interests, among other things. These systems often work in tandem with an ethics framework to help public officials avoid situations that may lead to conflicts of interest. In this case, disclosure agencies tend to build a closer relationship with public officials, as they prefer that officials consult the agency before the conflict takes place. To establish the necessary rapport with public officials, countries may have more than one disclosure agency—for example, a commission in the legislative branch, another in the judiciary, and one devoted to the executive.

Many of the newer disclosure systems that focus on conflicts of interest prioritize identifying actual conflicts and imposing sanctions. These systems also tend to allocate limited resources to prevention and to collaboration with public officials.

Despite the differing objectives of systems that focus on illicit wealth and of systems that focus on conflicts of interest, many countries seek to implement systems that incorporate elements of both types (figure 1.3). A combined system allows for a broader range of anticorruption objectives but requires a more comprehensive regulatory framework and more resources. Thus, when opting for systems designed to tackle both unexplained variations in wealth and conflicts of interest, countries should take extra care to understand the system requirements and to ensure that objectives are handled appropriately. For example, a combined system not only requires that disclosure forms request comprehensive information on both assets and interests, it also requires developing the capacity of disclosure agency practitioners to analyze the information.

The data collected by the team reveal that systems focused on illicit wealth are more common in developing countries, whereas COI systems are more common in countries belonging to the Organisation for Economic Co-operation and Development (OECD). There are several reasons for this discrepancy. First, the nexus between illicit enrichment and corrupt activities is more evident; one can often draw a straight line between illicit funds and corruption. The connection between conflicts of interest and corruption, however, is usually more nuanced. Second, COI systems are primarily preventive in that they are designed to identify and prevent potential conflicts, whereas illicit enrichment systems deter corrupt activity and are more punitive in nature.

FIGURE 1.3 Systems Combine Elements of Both Illicit Wealth and Conflicts of Interest Objectives

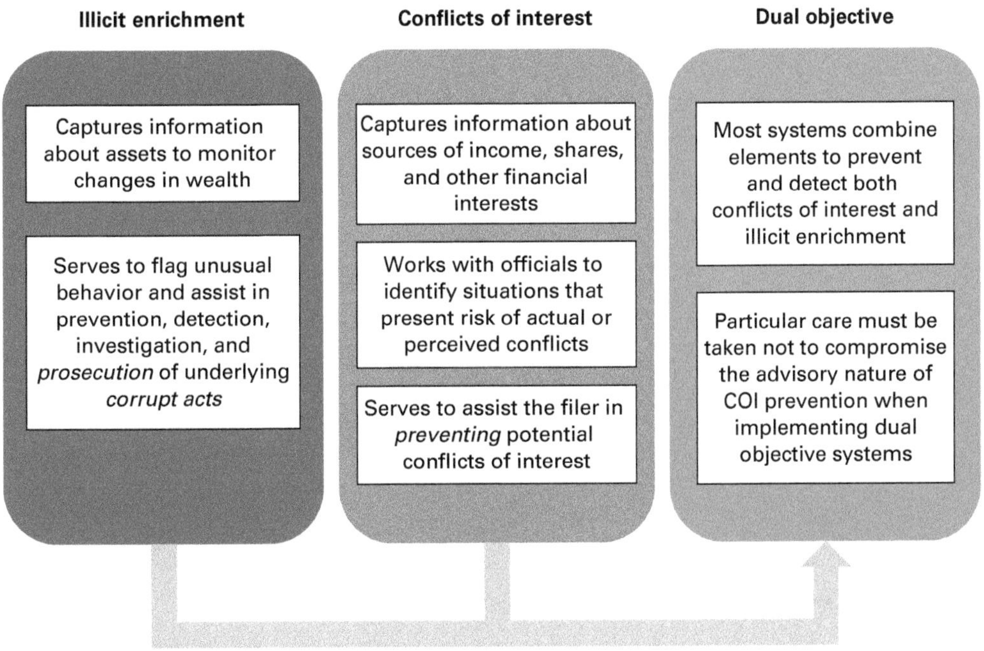

Illicit enrichment

- Captures information about assets to monitor changes in wealth
- Serves to flag unusual behavior and assist in prevention, detection, investigation, and *prosecution* of underlying corrupt acts

Conflicts of interest

- Captures information about sources of income, shares, and other financial interests
- Works with officials to identify situations that present risk of actual or perceived conflicts
- Serves to assist the filer in *preventing* potential conflicts of interest

Dual objective

- Most systems combine elements to prevent and detect both conflicts of interest and illicit enrichment
- Particular care must be taken not to compromise the advisory nature of COI prevention when implementing dual objective systems

Source: StAR 2012, 11.

When faced with a corruption scandal or questions of integrity in its public sector, it is better perceived to take action to remedy the situation by catching and prosecuting corrupt officials than it is to implement measures to prevent future infractions. The fact that COI systems are often overlooked or underdeveloped as anticorruption tools is a significant issue, and though this guide does not delve more deeply into the challenges of COI systems, it is a topic that merits further study and action.

Legal Foundations of Disclosure Systems

The legal foundations of disclosure systems are both domestic and international.

Domestic Legal Foundations

The legal framework of an effective financial disclosure system must be set in and reinforce a country's broader legal norms that mandate public officials to uphold certain standards of accountability and ethics. These norms are commonly set out in administrative, civil, criminal, or status laws (for example, laws on the status of members of parliament) and in codes of ethics.

Provisions that require disclosures of public officials are generally included in a comprehensive set of anticorruption laws or are adopted as standalone legislation or as codes of conduct. Regardless of how they are incorporated, the laws should, most importantly, provide *sufficient legal foundation* for the financial disclosure system while also allowing the system enough *flexibility* to respond to new challenges and to adapt to changes in resources.[6]

International Conventions and Other Instruments

Inclusion of disclosure principles and guidelines in international instruments has grown steadily in recent years, providing useful leverage for many governments to undertake comprehensive and sometimes politically risky reforms.

The UNCAC, adopted in 2003, includes provisions for establishing anticorruption bodies and for enhancing transparency in public service. Specific to financial disclosure, article 8, paragraph 5, states the following:

> Each State Party shall endeavor, where appropriate and in accordance with the fundamental principles of its domestic law, to establish measures and systems requiring public officials to make declarations to appropriate authorities regarding, inter alia, their outside activities, employment, investments, assets and substantial gifts or benefits from which a conflict of interest may result with respect to their functions as public officials.

In addition to the article above, further emphasis on the need for financial disclosures appears in article 52, paragraph 5, which states the following:

> Each State Party shall consider establishing, in accordance with its domestic law, effective financial disclosure systems for appropriate public officials and shall provide for appropriate

sanctions for non-compliance. Each State Party shall also consider taking such measures as may be necessary to permit its competent authorities to share that information with the competent authorities in other States Parties when necessary to investigate, claim and recover proceeds of offences established in accordance with this Convention.

These articles are binding on all of the 178 states that are currently party to the convention, and their implementation will be assessed as part of the second cycle of reviews under the UNCAC implementation review mechanism.[7]

These two articles—in addition to provisions addressing disclosure; conflicts of interest; and similar anticorruption measures in the Inter-American Convention against Corruption (IACAC),[8] the African Union Convention against Corruption (AUCC),[9] and the OECD Convention on Combating Bribery of Foreign Public Officials[10]— serve as the international basis for financial disclosure. Although these conventions clearly lay out the financial disclosure framework, disclosure of assets and interests, unlike other related disciplines such as anti-money-laundering and antibribery, does not have an internationally agreed on set of guidelines for implementation.[11] Some regional and international documents, however, do provide valuable guidance on the subject.

In 2012, recognizing the growing role and importance of financial disclosure in the international anticorruption dialogue, leaders of the Asia-Pacific Economic Cooperation (APEC) agreed on APEC's high-level principles on financial disclosure by public officials (APEC 2012). Later that year, G-20 members also endorsed common principles on financial disclosure, recognizing it as a powerful tool for holding governments accountable and for preventing conflicts of interest and corruption (G-20 2012). Figure 1.4 shows a timeline for adoption of international measures.

In May 2014, officials in charge of financial disclosure from 16 countries in West and Central Africa met in Dakar, Senegal, for the Regional Conference on Asset Disclosure. The purpose of the meeting was to (a) provide an overview of pertinent laws, (b) share technical experiences in the collection and verification of financial disclosures, (c) adopt guidelines, and (d) develop a research and advocacy strategy to enhance current financial disclosure systems. The result of this meeting was the Dakar Declaration on Asset Disclosure,[12] which includes a series of financial disclosure recommendations for the region. Similarly, representatives of an initiative led by the Balkan countries and the Regional School of Public Administration gathered in 2014 in Vilnius, Lithuania, to review the Balkan countries' financial disclosure practices. This regional meeting led to the Western Balkan Recommendation on Disclosure of Finances and Interests by Public Officials,[13] which includes guidelines for financial disclosure implementation.

These international instruments and initiatives provide information on good practices, recommendations, and principles that help countries seeking to implement financial disclosure laws. What was once seen primarily as a domestic issue is now regarded as an international concern of utmost importance—and one that has a clear

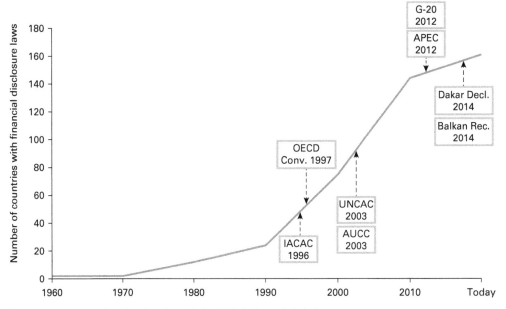

FIGURE 1.4 International Anticorruption Instruments and Adoption of Financial Disclosure Laws

Note: Approximate numbers based on the analysis of 158 disclosure jurisdictions.

nexus with anticorruption and asset recovery measures. Thus, as the global fight against corruption intensifies, the implementation of effective disclosure systems will also become more prominent.

Expectations: The Nonlegal Key to Successful Objectives

When designing and implementing a financial disclosure system, managing expectations is a necessary and often underestimated element and indicator of the ultimate effectiveness and credibility of a financial disclosure system. Financial disclosure systems are powerful tools, but they are also prone to disappointing results and setbacks if they are launched with overly ambitious mandates, are not supported by adequate resources, or are not underpinned by political commitment.

> Setting realistic expectations is crucial to establishing an effective and credible system: disclosure alone cannot combat corruption.

Realistic expectations also include honest views of a disclosure system's projected impact. Financial disclosure can help detect corrupt behavior or prevent conflicts of interest, but disclosure alone cannot combat corruption. Financial disclosure measures need to be integrated into a larger anticorruption framework.

Identifying and prioritizing the objectives of a financial disclosure system require similar pragmatism. Being realistic from the outset about objectives and expectations goes a long way toward establishing credibility and a culture of integrity. Unlike other anticorruption mechanisms, financial disclosure simultaneously addresses both prevention and detection, which allows for casting a very wide net. But broader is not always better, especially if the resources and political support are not there to support such a mandate. To maximize the effectiveness of disclosure systems, countries should prioritize their objectives.

In summary, realistic expectations are critical for the success of a financial disclosure system. Disclosures may help prevent corruption, but they are not a silver bullet—especially in countries where corruption is widespread, tax systems are dysfunctional, or law enforcement is weak. Nonetheless, a well-designed and operational system of financial disclosures can be an important element in a country's overall anticorruption framework.

Chapter 1—Key Recommendations

- Regardless of the different reasons countries have for developing disclosure systems, practitioners should see such systems as opportunities to work toward positive outcomes (for example, greater integrity in public service and a strengthened fight against corruption).

- Although simply adopting a financial disclosure law may appear to meet requirements set forth in international instruments, countries should work toward effective implementation of the law.

- Many financial disclosure systems share an overall objective to create a culture of integrity, but each system should be designed to target a given country's specific objectives (for example, detection and prevention of illicit wealth, prevention of conflicts of interest, or a combination of objectives).

- A successful disclosure system's objectives should be delineated in some form of domestic law and should be associated with specific processes (for example, providing guidance to officials to identify potential conflicts of interest).

- Expectations for a successful disclosure system must be realistic; disclosure alone cannot combat corruption.

Notes

1. The break-in at the Democratic National Committee headquarters at the Watergate office complex in Washington, DC, in 1972, commonly known as the Watergate scandal, turned out to be a key point in the development of financial disclosure frameworks. U.S. President Richard Nixon resigned in 1974, and the Ethics in

Government Act was enacted in 1978. For more information, visit http://www.oge
.gov/FOIA-and-Privacy-Act/The-Ethics-in-Government-Act/The-Ethics-in
-Government-Act/.

2. Article 8, paragraph 5, of the UNCAC establishes that "Each State Party shall
   endeavor, where appropriate and in accordance with the fundamental principles of
   its domestic law, to establish measures and systems requiring public officials to
   make declarations to appropriate authorities regarding, inter alia, their outside
   activities, employment, investments, assets and substantial gifts or benefits from
   which a conflict of interest may result with respect to their functions as public officials." For the full text of the convention, see https://www.unodc.org/documents
   /treaties/UNCAC/Publications/Convention/08-50026_E.pdf.

3. See the section in this chapter titled "Legal Foundations of Disclosure Systems" for
   more information on international instruments.

4. In 2013–14, at least seven countries added new financial disclosure laws, and a
   few—such as France—did major overhauls of their systems.

5. *Technical Guide to the United Nations Convention against Corruption*, Vienna,
   Austria, 25, http://www.unodc.org/documents/corruption/Technical_Guide_UNCAC
   .pdf. See also UNCAC Article 7 (4), "Each State Party shall, in accordance with the
   fundamental principles of its domestic law, endeavour to adopt, maintain and strengthen
   systems that promote transparency and prevent conflicts of interest."; UNCAC
   Article 8(5);UNCAC Article 7(4); 8(3); 52(5)(6); GA/RES/51/59 9 I c, 12 II e.

6. For more on the nexus between financial disclosure laws and regulatory systems, see
   StAR (2012).

7. The Conference of the States Parties to the UNCAC decided to establish a mandatory
   review mechanism for all states parties. Resolution 3/1 of the conference adopted the
   terms of reference of the mechanism for the review of implementation of the UNCAC
   and set out the goals of the review process, which include the promotion of the purposes of the UNCAC as well as the provision of information on its implementation.
   The work of the mechanism is run by the Implementation Review Group, which
   overviews the review process to identify challenges and good practices and to consider technical assistance requirements. Each country review process starts with the
   compilation of a self-assessment report. States then engage in dialogue with their
   peer reviewers, and this process may entail a country visit. A country review report
   and executive summary are prepared in the final stage. These documents enable an
   overall aggregate analysis of how the UNCAC is being implemented globally.
   Information on the implementation of article 20 on illicit enrichment has already
   been gathered under the first cycle of review, and countries have provided relevant
   information on their AD systems in this context.

8. Adopted by the Organization of American States in 1996, the IACAC, in article III,
   requires that states "create, maintain, and strengthen … systems for registering the
   income, assets, and liabilities of persons who perform public functions in certain
   posts as specified by law."

9. Adopted by the African Union in 2003, the AUCC, in article 7, requires that states
   commit themselves to "require all or designated public officials to declare their
   assets at the time of assumption of office during and after their term of office in the
   public service."

10. The OECD convention is the first anticorruption instrument focused on the supply side of corruption. Although it does not include a specific provision regarding financial disclosure, systems that help monitor changes in the wealth of public officials can assist in the enforcement of the convention.

11. In contrast, the International Standards on Combating Money Laundering and the Financing of Terrorism and Proliferation, adopted by the Financial Action Task Force on Money Laundering, establish a comprehensive framework of measures for signatory countries to implement in order to combat money laundering, terrorist financing, and financing of proliferation of weapons of mass destruction. See FATF (2012).

12. The text of the declaration is available at https://www.unodc.org/documents /corruption/WG-Prevention/Art_8_Financial_disclosure_declaration_of_assets /Declaration_de_Dakar_fr.pdf.

13. This document is available at http://www.respaweb.eu/11/library#respa-publications -and-research-18.

References

APEC (Asia-Pacific Economic Cooperation). 2012. "APEC Principles for Financial/ Asset Disclosure by Public Officials: Fundamentals for an Effective Tool to Prevent, Detect, and Prosecute Conflicts of Interest, Illicit Enrichment, and Other Forms of Corruption." Submitted by the United States at the 14th Anticorruption and Transparency Experts' Working Group Meeting, Moscow, February 2–3. http:// mddb.apec.org/documents/2012/ACT/ACT1/12_act1_002.doc.

FATF (Financial Action Task Force). 2012. *International Standards on Combating Money Laundering and the Financing of Terrorism and Proliferation*. Paris: FATF. http://www.fatf-gafi.org/media/fatf/documents/recommendations/pdfs/FATF _Recommendations.pdf.

G-20 (Group of 20). 2012. "High-Level Principles on Asset Disclosure by Public Officials." Adopted at the G-20 Leaders' Summit, Los Cabos, Mexico, June 18–19. http://star.worldbank.org/star/sites/star/files/los_cabos_2012_high_level_principles _on_asset_disclosure.pdf.

StAR (Stolen Asset Recovery Initiative). 2012. *Public Office, Private Interests: Accountability through Income and Asset Disclosure*. Washington, DC: World Bank.

UNODC (United Nations Office on Drugs and Crime). 2009. *Technical Guide to the United Nations Convention against Corruption*. Vienna: UNODC. http://www.unodc .org/documents/corruption/Technical_Guide_UNCAC.pdf.

2. Who Should File a Disclosure? How Often?

This chapter provides an overview of current disclosure practices and presents a set of practical considerations that are often overlooked.

Who Should File a Disclosure?

Who should declare? There is no single answer, and—more importantly—answers may change with developments over time. Discussions of who should declare generally reflect two options: some countries require all public officials to file a disclosure, whereas others extend the obligation to only a narrower set of public officials.

Reasons for a broader disclosure mandate in which most or all public officials are required to declare include, among others, the possibility that corruption may occur at all levels of public service, and the desire to send a strong message to society about efforts to promote transparency. Depending on the definition of "public official" and the size of a country's public service population, a requirement encompassing all public officials could translate into hundreds, thousands, or even millions of filers, from the president of a country to the teacher of a rural school.

At the other end of the spectrum are reasons for a more targeted approach to disclosure. From corruption risk analysis to cost-effectiveness calculations, concerns about capacity to administer broad disclosure mandates, cultural and political resistance to disclosure, and even policy makers' personal motivations to remain exempt from disclosure can all lead to a more targeted mandate of who should declare. Such a narrower mandate can be organized by state branch (for example, only officials in the executive branch declare), type of appointment, responsibility, hierarchy, function, salary, or a combination of criteria.

Valid reasons exist for both broader and narrower mandates, so how should a country determine which public officials should declare? A useful approach to answering this question is focusing on *effectiveness* and *impact*. This could mean targeting those officials who are more relevant for the financial disclosure

> Focus on those officials who will be more relevant to effectively accomplishing disclosure goals.

system in terms of both effectively accomplishing its goals and maximizing its impact—thereby promoting ethics and transparency and curbing corruption.

As with many recommendations, this is easier said than done; however, we have some useful tips that can help guide the decision-making process and provide some practical perspective on this question.

Targeted Categories of Officials

A quick look at the global variation in disclosure requirements reveals a trend to include a wide range of public officials, including representatives from all branches of government and even local and regional officials. However, this does not mean that *all* public officials in *all* branches of government are required to declare. A closer look at the variation shows that some categories of officials are more frequently required to declare than are others, so there are indeed targeted approaches within the broader mandate (figure 2.1).

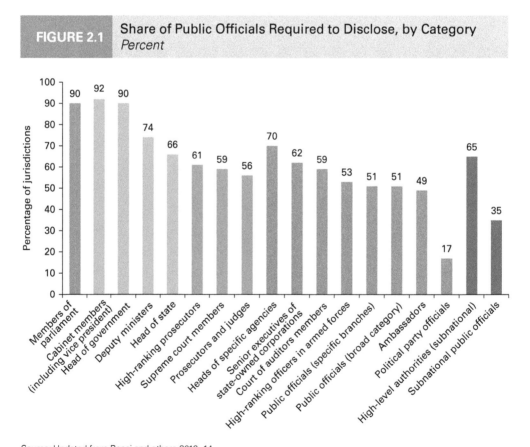

FIGURE 2.1 Share of Public Officials Required to Disclose, by Category
Percent

Source: Updated from Rossi and others 2012, 14.
Note: Different colored bars correspond to different branches/levels of government. Approximate percentages based on the analysis of 158 disclosure jurisdictions.

To determine who should declare, it is important to have very clear guidelines on how officials are selected. Some of the most common criteria include the following:

- Branch of government: identifying filers by their branch of government (executive branch, legislative branch, judicial branch, subnational government, local government, and so on)
- Hierarchy: identifying filers by their hierarchical level (for example, all officials at the director level and above)
- Position: identifying filers by their title (minister, deputy minister, director, and so on)
- Function: identifying filers by the type of activity they perform (administrative decision making, granting contracts, public procurement, tax inspection, customs, and so on)
- Risk of corruption: identifying filers based upon their role and the risk they could become involved in corrupt activity, which requires a prior assessment of the most common forms of corruption in the country (building licenses, infrastructure contracts, customs, and so on)
- Classification as a politically exposed person (PEP): identifying and including filers who are classified as PEPs in the AML/CFT (anti-money-laundering and combating the financing of terrorism) laws of the country. This may increase the utility of the financial disclosure system to support "Know Your Customer" (KYC) due diligence requirements of anti-money-laundering and financing of terrorism systems.

Determining which public officials will file could entail one, several, or all of these criteria. Once the criteria have been selected, it is useful to consider two questions:

- Are all relevant categories of officials included within the selected criteria? For example, if a country chooses hierarchy as the primary criterion, are there any officials below the chosen level who should still be targeted because they work either in areas that pose a high risk of corruption or in critical sectors such as banking or natural resources?
- Are there categories of officials for which disclosure might not be the most effective tool? For example, it may not be cost-effective to require disclosure in situations where officials have limited opportunities to engage in corruption or where the concerns involve possible petty corruption.

Regardless of the objective criteria selected by a country, they should allow for easy identification of all positions required to file. For this reason, it is very useful to select a clear and specific set of criteria that minimizes the need for subjective interpretation. For example, what does "high level" mean? Is such a designation to be determined by rank, by salary scale, or by some other measure?

> Criteria for targeting officials should allow for easy identification of all positions required to file.

In many cases, although the need for subjective interpretation of the criteria can be minimized, it cannot be completely eliminated. Thus, it is important to determine who will be responsible for the interpretation and to provide sufficient resources for that person or entity to perform this analysis. Whoever is responsible for interpreting the criteria must be able to act with both independence and objectivity. The credibility of the entire system will be undermined if the person responsible for interpreting the criteria is believed to have had ulterior motives when drawing up the list of filers. Furthermore, declaring is often seen as a burden by public officials, so discovering that this burden is not equally shared by colleagues in similar positions would likely result in displeasure and distrust in the system.

Put a Name to It: Creating and Updating a List of Filers

Identifying the positions that are required to declare is only half of the process. The names of the officials occupying those positions also need to be determined. Some government positions may be very

> Identifying the positions is only half of the process.

stable over time, whereas others may change frequently; consider elections, promotions, people on leave, and officials acting for others, and it becomes clear that a country's list of filers will be quite dynamic. In other words, a list of actual filers is only a "snapshot" of a particular point in time and needs to be updated with certain regularity.

Building a list of actual filers can be quite challenging, and sometimes it may be unrealistic to try to build a centralized one. Approximately 65 percent of the disclosure jurisdictions in the sample built a centralized list of filers to ensure compliance, and the remaining jurisdictions found alternative ways.

Some of the challenges that may arise when trying to build a list of filers include lack of the following: (a) human resources (HR) offices, (b) centralized personnel information for the public sector, (c) up-to-date personnel information for the public sector, (d) communication between financial disclosure officials and HR offices, and (e) resources for HR offices to gather up-to-date data.

This inability to draw up a list of filers may have a very negative impact on the financial disclosure system. If an agency does not know who is supposed to file, how can agency officials inform public officials of their duties? How can agency officials check compliance rates? Such issues, which may seem merely administrative, can erode credibility and trust in the financial disclosure system.

Thus, if a country is aware of objective challenges that are preventing the creation of a list of filers, it is imperative that the country tackle those challenges with creativity from point zero. Not addressing these challenges guarantees limited capacity to implement the system and dooms it from the start.

Size Matters

A common challenge in the implementation of financial disclosure systems is the absence of dialogue when drafting the law between the policy makers and the practitioners who will implement the system. Such a challenge may also be viewed as a difference between the intention of the system and its realization. Many countries have adopted countless financial disclosure laws that clearly delineate criteria for officials who are required to declare, but without considering how many filers those criteria include or the resources needed to manage filers' information. Recent research shows the large variation in terms of numbers of filers (figure 2.2).

As figure 2.2 shows, 28 percent of the countries in the sample have between 10,000 and 50,000 filers, but the remaining 72 percent are quite evenly distributed between hundreds of filers and millions of them. Intuition would suggest that the number of filers might correlate with variables such as the branches of government covered by disclosure

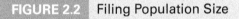

FIGURE 2.2 Filing Population Size

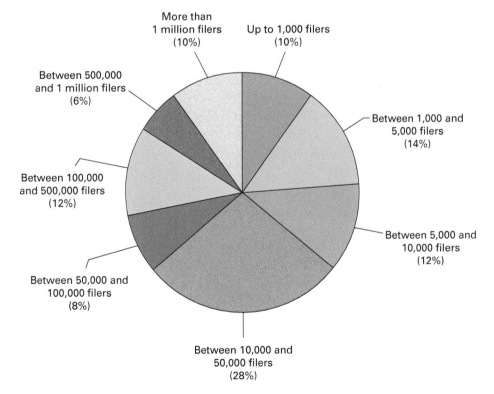

Note: Approximate percentages based on the analysis of 52 disclosure jurisdictions.

requirements, the size of the public sector, or even the population of a country. However, this is not always the case. For instance, both Albania and the Republic of Korea cover all branches of government. Although these countries have very different populations in terms of size—Albania's population is 2.89 million, and Korea's is 50.42 million, according to 2014 data from the World Bank—they have a very similar number of filers. This example suggests that there is no easy formula to predict or even calculate the appropriate size of the filing population in any jurisdiction.

In our experience, a useful approach is to do a realistic analysis of the volume of disclosures that a financial disclosure agency can actually manage while fulfilling its objectives effectively. In other words, if a financial disclosure agency has two dedicated staff members, and the law defines one million filers, will two people and their available resources be enough to support the filers, receive the disclosures, screen the disclosures, provide access, exchange information with other agencies, detect irregularities, and carry out any other activities that the law may mandate? Probably not.[1]

Targeting the correct officials is one half of the equation for achieving a system's objectives; the other is ensuring that the volume of disclosures to be received in each cycle is manageable. The number of filers will affect every step of the disclosure process, as well as its effectiveness (see figure 2.3).

FIGURE 2.3   Size of Disclosure Population

Size of disclosure population matters

Needs to be aligned with resources and capacity of disclosure agency

Affects

| Collection | Compliance | Verification | Imposing sanctions |

Therefore, although lawmakers may have the best intentions when thinking of how to define potential filers, it is important not to forget that an unmanageable number of filers may hamper all possibilities of success for a financial disclosure system.

Family Members

Approximately 65 percent of countries with disclosure laws—in particular, as figure 2.4 shows, the lower-middle- and upper-middle-income economies—require officials to submit information not only for themselves but also for their family members. The definition

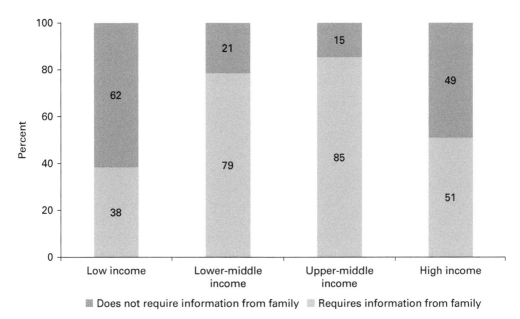

FIGURE 2.4 Share of Jurisdictions Requiring Disclosure of Family Members

Legend: ■ Does not require information from family ■ Requires information from family

Note: Approximate percentages based on the analysis of 158 disclosure jurisdictions.

of "family members" and the information requested from them varies from country to country. However, this percentage shows that a large number of countries consider it relevant to have information not only from public officials, but also from their relatives.

> Family members should be included in disclosure requirements.

As figure 2.4 shows, lower-middle- and upper-middle-income economies in particular require information on family members.

Officials may misuse public office and attempt to hide illicit wealth through their family members to circumvent oversight mechanisms.[2] Indeed, under AML/CFT standards,[3] the definition of PEPs—who are considered at greater risk of engaging in money laundering, as they may abuse their position and influence to carry out corrupt acts—includes the family members and close associates of those individuals who are or who have been entrusted with prominent public functions.[4]

The term "family members" is generally understood to include the filer's spouse and children. However, a country's cultural and legal context may broaden that definition to include other relatives, dependents living in the same household, or domestic partners who are not legally married, to name just a few alternatives.

The way the information is requested also varies greatly from country to country. Whereas some countries may require a filer to include family members' asset information only if those assets are jointly held with the public official, others may require family members to submit a separate form declaring all assets held, regardless of whether the filer is a co-owner.

Theory and practice show the importance of considering the inclusion of family members in disclosure requirements. The main concern then becomes what and how much information should be collected (this concern is addressed in chapter 3). As previously discussed, an important challenge for most countries is finding the right balance between coverage and a manageable size for the filing population. Collecting information on family members affects this balance, as doing so may indirectly increase the number of filers and may significantly increase the amount of information that the agency must process for each filer.

At a minimum, therefore, it is important that disclosure forms require enough information to fully identify all family members as they are defined by a country. Decisions about the amount of information requested from family members follow the same rule as that for public officials, which seeks to find a balance between the relevance of that information to the system's objectives and the capacity of the agency to process that information (see chapter 3). In the case of family members, it is also important to consider privacy laws, especially if the information in the disclosure forms is made publicly available.

How Often Should Filers Declare?

Settling the issue of who should declare is only the beginning. How often officials must submit their disclosures still needs to be decided.

The most common answers to the questions on frequency are as follows: upon entering office, upon leaving office, yearly, once every two years, upon experiencing significant changes in wealth, and upon emergence of a potential conflict of interest.

As figure 2.5 shows, 75 percent of the disclosure countries require officials to disclose their assets and liabilities more than twice per term in office. These countries also require officials to submit new forms upon experiencing any changes in their assets. Approximately 18 percent of countries require officials to disclose their assets and liabilities twice per term. Only 7 percent of jurisdictions require officials to file just once per term.

Filing frequency has many implications for a financial disclosure agency and for public officials. For an agency, the most obvious reasons for choosing a higher frequency are having current information and the ability to perform analysis across time. A higher frequency can also help build a culture of compliance, as officials are more frequently reminded of their obligation to declare. However, an often-overlooked aspect of frequency is that it affects how collection cycles will be organized.

> An often-overlooked aspect of frequency is that it also deeply affects how collection cycles will be organized.

FIGURE 2.5 | Frequency of Disclosure Requirements

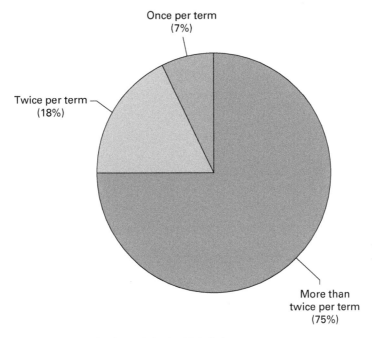

Note: Approximate percentages based on the analysis of 153 jurisdictions.

For example, in one country, public officials must declare on a yearly basis (around the time of their birthday). This means that the financial disclosure agency receives disclosures 365 days a year. In another country, public officials must declare on a yearly basis by a specific calendar date (around May). Both types of countries receive disclosures on a yearly basis, but their internal organization for managing the submission and compliance process is very different. One type receives disclosures on a rolling basis, whereas the other concentrates receipt around a certain date, thus creating a larger volume of work around that deadline.

Therefore, frequency affects not only how up to date the information is, but also how the financial disclosure agency needs to manage its resources. Frequency also affects volume, as how frequently an official must declare determines the number of disclosures to be received from that official.

In addition, frequency affects how burdensome disclosure requirements will be for filers. For instance, if a person must declare on a yearly basis, as well as every time a potential conflict of interest arises, how many times a year will the person need to file? Or, if an official must declare after every change in position, including when acting on behalf of his or her superior, would that require the official to declare, for example, on a monthly basis?

As straightforward as filing frequency may seem, its various elements can clearly have a significant impact on both the filer and the capacity of the agency. Therefore, although it is undoubtedly better for an official to declare more than twice per term, just how many times an official should declare is yet another important aspect that needs practical consideration.

Chapter 2—Key Recommendations

- The determination of who declares should depend on the disclosure goals of a given system and should focus on the types of officials relevant to those goals.

- The criteria for targeting officials—by branches of government, hierarchy, position, function, or risk of corruption—should be defined clearly enough to allow for easy identification of the positions covered.

- Identifying the positions is only half of the process; the list of filers must be populated with the names of officials occupying those positions.

- The filing population should be manageable in size and should include filers' family members. The size of the filing population should align with the financial disclosure agency's resources and capacity.

- Serious consideration should be given to the trade-offs involved in mandating disclosure for officials who have a low risk of corruption.

- A higher frequency of disclosure that requires officials to declare more than twice per term in office is preferable.

Notes

1. For more on this topic, see StAR (2012), 35.
2. For more on this discussion, please see StAR (2012), 36.
3. Please see http://www.fatf-gafi.org/publications/fatfrecommendations/documents/fatf -recommendations.html.
4. For more on PEPs, please see Greenberg and others (2010).

References

Greenberg, T., L. Gray, D. Schantz, M. Latham, and C. Garder. 2010. "Politically Exposed Persons: A Policy Paper on Strengthening Preventive Measures for the Banking Sector." World Bank, Washington, DC.

Rossi, I., L. Pop, F. Clementucci, and L. Sawaqed. 2012. "Using Asset Disclosure for Identifying Politically Exposed Persons." World Bank, Washington, DC.

StAR (Stolen Asset Recovery Initiative). 2012. *Public Office, Private Interests: Accountability through Income and Asset Disclosure*. Washington, DC: World Bank.

3. What to Declare?

An early version of an interest disclosure form read, "Please declare all your interests," and provided a large blank space to be filled in by the public official. Upon analyzing the forms received by public officials, financial disclosure staff members noticed the different interpretations that each filer had given to the same guidance. Whereas one senator detailed every company he had an interest in, the number of shares, and their value, another filer simply wrote, "I have agricultural interests."

The answer to the question of what to declare is often found in the disclosure legislation, but, in all cases, a more detailed answer is always available in the blank disclosure form. Sometimes in paper formats but increasingly in electronic ones, the disclosure form is what public officials must fill out in order to comply with disclosure requirements. This means that the content of the disclosure form is the main and most important input in making the financial disclosure system work.

The disclosure form also represents the public official's primary interaction with the disclosure agency and the overall system. This means that the disclosure form sets the tone for this interaction and for the overall perception that filers have of the system itself. Reactions can range from annoyance toward a burdensome obligation to frustration, confusion, and even mistrust.

> The blank form is the main and most important input of the disclosure system, and the filers' primary interaction with it.

The financial disclosure form is therefore a fundamental piece of the disclosure system puzzle. In other words, if legislation is the system's foundation, the form is the key to open the front door.

A weak form can compromise a system that has solid legislation, an optimal number of filers, an effective filing and data management system, and appropriate tools for ensuring compliance. A strong form ensures that the data gathered and all the resources invested in verification or public access can ultimately have an impact in terms of the accountability of public officials and the prevention and detection of corruption.

The information provided by officials through the form provides the starting point for all other processes, from determining compliance to analyzing unjustified variations of wealth or conflicts of interest. In countries that make information from financial disclosures public, the information also affects the perceptions of transparency that civil society, the public, and the media may have. The form serves as both the entry point and the focal point of the disclosure system.

What Makes a Disclosure Form Strong or Weak?

A strong form is user friendly, asks for relevant information, and is balanced in terms of its comprehensiveness.

Filling out a disclosure form can be a stressful exercise. Personal information must be entered in a pre-established format. A user-friendly form ensures that the information requested is clear and easy to complete (figure 3.1). When a form is not user friendly, the quality of the data collected is compromised and filers are burdened unnecessarily. In those situations, the resources of financial disclosure agencies are wasted on following up on involuntary filing errors.

In the example in the figure, each field is clearly defined and even provides examples, making it easier for the filer to understand what information is needed. Furthermore, this form manages to request comprehensive information on income—covering type, source, and value—in a very simple format.

Uncertainty about how to fill out the form should be eliminated through careful design of the form. For example, if a filer must provide the value of an asset, the form should clarify whether it is the market value or the acquisition value. Otherwise,

FIGURE 3.1 Disclosure Form Example, Income

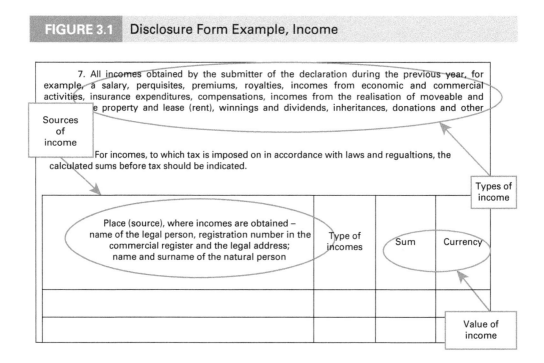

FIGURE 3.2	Disclosure Form Example, Unclear Request of Value of Assets

Assets (as of the statement date)

(Including, but not limited to, land, buildings, vehicles, investments, and financial obligations owed to the person for whom the statement is made.)

Description (include location of asset where applicable)	Approximate value

as in the example in figure 3.2, the filer is unsure whether he or she has indicated the correct value, and the financial disclosure agency does not know which value to use for verification purposes.

The excessive use of open-ended questions on forms can add an unmanageable layer of complexity. For example, a form that asks how a property was acquired and provides a blank section for the explanation can be confusing for the filer. Should the filer include one word ("inheritance") or write four lines about the circumstances of the inheritance?

Making the transition from a paper-based to an electronic system does not decrease the importance of user friendliness and good form design. Electronic filing (e-filing) creates great opportunities in terms of data processing and monitoring. However, these opportunities cannot be fully realized without proper attention to details, such as creating drop-down menus for different types of real estate as opposed to blank fields, which open the door for misspellings (for example, of the word *garage*). Moreover, all of the scenarios described earlier are not magically eliminated when forms are filed electronically.

Requesting relevant information means asking for information that will actually contribute to achieving the objectives of the system. For example, if the objective is to identify conflicts of interest, the disclosure of positions in companies and of outside activities should be a priority. In systems that have as their objective monitoring variations of wealth, the focus should be on assets and income.

> The information requested in the declaration form needs to reflect the objectives of the system.

A weak form requires either too much or too little information (see figure 3.3.). Both scenarios are suboptimal. Requesting too much information can become a burden for the filer while bringing no added benefits to the institutions managing the system. The disclosure agency may not have sufficient capacity for analyzing and processing the

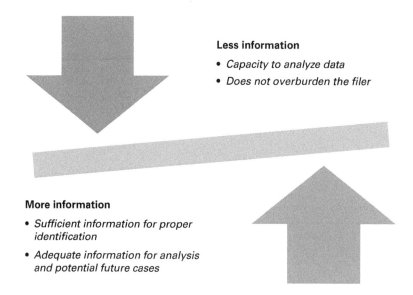

Less information
- *Capacity to analyze data*
- *Does not overburden the filer*

More information
- *Sufficient information for proper identification*
- *Adequate information for analysis and potential future cases*

data it collects. Requesting too little information can jeopardize the ability of the system to achieve its objectives by not shedding sufficient light on high-risk aspects of an official's assets or interests. A weak form is also disconnected from the objectives of the system. For example, in a country where financial disclosure is expected to help manage potential conflicts of interest, a weak form might focus on less relevant items such as real estate.

Finding the right balance is not easy and may take several iterations of the disclosure form. In many countries, after several years of using a disclosure form that had initially appeared to satisfy the principles of user friendliness, relevance, and balance, practitioners have concluded that their forms require amendment. The causes for this conclusion can be many. For example, numerous filers might find sections of the form unclear. There might be changes in external factors, such as new asset classes (for example, virtual currencies), or asset types newly identified as potential money-laundering vehicles (for example, art), or technological changes in the system that allow for easier processing of information. Staff members working in financial disclosure agencies might also find that the information in the form does not allow them to monitor variations of wealth effectively or to advise officials on managing conflict of interest situations. Because the form needs to be tailored to the system's country-specific corruption risks and context (for example, approaches to land and property ownership, complexity of financial instruments most commonly used, use of cash, appropriate thresholds, and so on), it is a work in progress that needs regular reassessment and fine-tuning.

What Categories of Information Are Included in Financial Disclosure Forms?

The categories of information included in the financial disclosure need to reflect the objectives of the system. Globally, filers disclose a broad range of information. In order to visualize the menu of options, data have been collected on the main categories of information included in disclosures. The categories shown in table 3.1 are not exhaustive; for example, categories such as contracts with public sector entities are not included.

Most disclosure systems require filers to provide information on immovable assets (such as real estate), sources of income, stocks and securities, and business relationships with financial institutions (that is, bank accounts). Table 3.1 also shows regional preferences. For example, disclosure systems in high-income countries belonging to the Organisation for Economic Co-operation and Development (OECD) place more emphasis on categories such as high-level positions, unpaid activities, and posttenure activities relative to other regions. This is explained by the fact that the primary objective in OECD disclosure systems is preventing and managing conflicts of interest.

Globally, fewer systems focus on collecting information about high-level positions outside the public sector or about posttenure activities. The data in table 3.1 show that the categories of information that focus on the financial side of disclosure are more widespread at a global level than are those that focus on conflict of interest aspects. The reason is that more systems globally focus on illicit enrichment than on conflicts of interest. For those that focus on both, the financial aspects tend to be included more frequently than are the conflicts of interest ones.

However, the information in table 3.1 does not tell the whole story, as the depth and breadth of requirements can also largely vary. The fact that 87 percent of OECD high-income countries require the disclosure of securities does not mean that they all require the same information. In fact, 53 percent of OECD high-income countries declare both the value and the name of the entity in which securities are held; the rest focus on either the value of the securities or the name of the company (figure 3.4).

Furthermore, the categories of information are only the headlines of the disclosure. If the system's objective is to detect illicit enrichment, requesting filers to declare real estate or immovable assets is just the first step. Translating that decision into a section or a field in a form is a more complicated step. Should filers provide the market value, the acquisition value, or both? Should they provide the plot identification number?

In the next section, we share some practices and experiences we have encountered in our analytical and advisory work on translating disclosure objectives into a form. This section was not designed as an exhaustive guide to the different components of the financial disclosure form. From our experience, not all components of a form present the same implementation challenges. Our approach reflects the realities that the challenges presented by blank forms evolve and that forms usually need regular fine-tuning.

Category	Global	Asia	Europe and Central Asia	Latin America and the Caribbean	Middle East and North Africa	OECD high-income	Sub-Saharan Africa
TABLE 3.1	**Categories of Information Typically Found in Disclosure Forms** *Percentage of countries*						
Immovable assets	88	100	90	100	82	78	80
Sources of income	77	73	95	96	45	100	48
Stocks and securities	86	100	95	100	64	87	70
Bank accounts	80	86	86	100	64	72	70
Cash	29	45	38	37	36	16	20
Values of income	67	73	90	93	27	63	48
Movable assets	80	86	90	100	82	56	75
Liabilities	72	82	71	100	45	56	68
Pretenure activities	58	45	71	85	27	75	33
High-level positions	41	45	38	33	27	84	15
Gifts	39	59	57	33	9	53	18
Other positions	30	32	19	19	36	69	10
Unpaid activities	29	18	38	22	9	69	10
Expenditures	18	18	38	22	0	25	3
Sponsored travel	14	14	5	4	0	41	8
Posttenure activities	14	0	29	7	0	34	8

Note: OECD = Organisation for Economic Co-operation and Development. Approximate percentages based on the analysis of 153 jurisdictions.

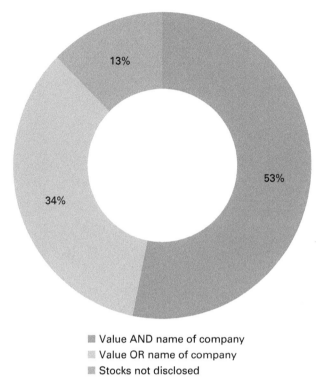

- ■ Value AND name of company
- ■ Value OR name of company
- ■ Stocks not disclosed

Note: OECD = Organisation for Economic Co-operation and Development. Approximate percentages based on the analysis of the 32 OECD high-income jurisdictions analyzed for this guide.

Personal Identification Information

Although we have noted the dangers of requesting too much information, with regard to personal information, more is actually better. Personal identification (ID) information can help distinguish between officials who share the same name. It is also useful for cross-checking with information from outside registries and databases. For instance, take the name of one of our authors, Laura Pop. A search on the website where disclosures are made public in Romania resulted in at least four filers with the same name. One is employed in the Road and Bridge Administration, two are on the regional council, and the fourth holds a position in a public procurement department. There are many other Laura Pops among the filers, but all of them have a middle name.[1]

> When it comes to personal information, more is actually better.

In addition to requesting the name of the official, the vast majority of disclosures request information on the filer's position, date of birth, or ID number. However, globally, only some countries require all three pieces of information (for a regional breakdown, see figure 3.5):

- 75 percent of jurisdictions require the filer's position; only 33 jurisdictions do not.
- 37 percent require an ID number, most commonly a national ID number or a fiscal ID number such as a tax registration or social security number.
- 31 percent require the filer's date of birth.
- Only 18 percent require all three—position, date of birth, and ID number.

How Is Identification Information Included?

Some countries require one form of identification, such as a tax ID number, ID card number, or personal ID number. In other countries, multiple forms of identification are requested.

ID numbers, date and place of birth, and ID information for family members can be particularly useful for cross-checking information with data from outside registries

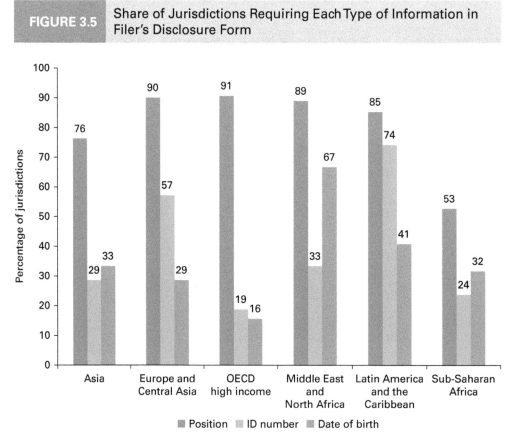

FIGURE 3.5 Share of Jurisdictions Requiring Each Type of Information in Filer's Disclosure Form

Note: ID = identification. Approximate percentages based on the analysis of 148 disclosure jurisdictions.

and databases. Information on a public official's position, job title, and grade, as well as professional responsibilities, can help determine the risk profile of the filer and whether that filer is a politically exposed person. For example, information on the position or job title can provide valuable information on the areas in which potential conflicts of interest might arise. For example, the nature of the conflict risk for a filer working in procurement will differ from that of a judge.

Declaring Immovable and Movable Assets

What Are Immovable and Movable Assets?

Requesting both immovable and movable assets is widespread across regions. The categories that are defined as immovable assets are quite consistent across disclosure systems:

- Real estate (commercial and residential)
- Land
  - In urban and rural areas
  - With different uses (such as farmland, pastures, lakes, and forests).

There is more variation with regard to movable assets. Vehicles (cars, ships, planes, helicopters, agricultural vehicles, and so on), jewelry, and precious metals are the most common. Some disclosure systems require detailed information on categories of livestock (sheep, cattle, goats, poultry, horses, and so on), as well as antiques, art, or gun collections.

Four key questions affect the disclosure of both immovable and movable assets:

- How does one *identify* the asset?
- How does one *express* the value of the asset?
- How, when, and where was the asset *acquired*?
- What is the *nature* of ownership?

Since these issues are common to both categories, they are addressed in the same section.

How Does One Identify the Asset?

This category of the form can include the full (or partial) address, the lot number, the property registry or cadastral number, the type of immovable asset (house, apartment, garage, farmland, forest, or commercial real estate), or the size of the asset. It is also useful to include information that will allow the financial disclosure agency to match the information declared by the filer with information in registries, databases, or other documents. With regard to movable assets, one piece of information that is usually requested is the registration number of vehicles, boats, aircraft, and agricultural machinery.

How Does One Express the Value of the Asset?

This represents one of the most challenging of the issues that need to be addressed in the financial disclosure form (see figure 3.6). It requires careful consideration in terms of local context, objectives of the system, and ease of retrieval of the information for filers. Forms generally request filers to provide the market value, the purchase value, the fiscal value, or the insured value of an asset.

One example that illustrates the trade-offs and complexity involved in including the appropriate asset value(s) is the use of market value. This topic generates heated debate among financial disclosure practitioners worldwide. How to express the value of an asset raises a number of practical challenges, both for filers and for institutions that use this information. From the perspective of the filer, providing the market value for real estate or land is challenging, as the value of these assets is in continuous flux and, in most cases, subjective. Some financial disclosure practitioners acknowledge that they had a hard time coming up with the market value to include on their own disclosures. Moreover, they also mention that the value they ultimately used in the form is not particularly useful, as it is a subjective assessment made by each filer.

From the perspective of disclosure agencies, the market value might also not be the most helpful value for identifying unjustified variations in wealth. Although the market value of an asset might increase disproportionately to an increase in income, this could be wholly justified by variations in the real estate market or other factors such as inflation. Moreover, the cross-checking of the market value provided by the filer would require an expert evaluation, which would be unsustainable for most systems that receive a high number of disclosures. In some cases, the purchase value or the taxable value might be relatively easier to manage and could better contribute to fulfilling the disclosure system's objective of identifying unjustified variations of wealth, as there might be a paper trail or documentation associated with those values.

In the case of movable assets, an important issue to consider is that of threshold. For example, it can be useful to make a distinction between a regular chair and a piece of antique furniture. One approach we have seen is indicating a cumulative monetary value for jewelry, art, and antiques to be declared—such as €5,000 or US$6,000, depending on the local context. A threshold can also be relevant when it comes to livestock.

FIGURE 3.6 Value of the Asset

How to express the *value* of the asset?

- Market value vs. purchase value vs. fiscal value vs. insured value
- Currency
- Identifying a threshold for disclosure

Declaring two sheep is not as relevant or useful as declaring hundreds or thousands of sheep. Yet we have seen cases in which filers would have to declare even very low numbers of domestic animals such as turkeys or chickens.

How, When, and Where Was the Asset Acquired?

If the focus of the financial disclosure system is to trace unjustified variations of wealth, it is important to require filers to include assets held domestically as well as abroad. Indicating the year when an asset was acquired can also help distinguish between assets acquired before the start of an official's public service and those acquired while in office or afterward. In most cases, the corruption risks associated with an asset purchased or inherited 20 years before an official held any public sector position differ from those associated with an asset acquired while in office or immediately after ending time in office. On a number of occasions, we have seen limited distinction being made between assets acquired close to the filer's time in office and assets acquired at a time when the filer would have had limited opportunity to be involved in any corrupt practices (for example, prior to government service).

Information on how an asset was acquired (purchase, inheritance, gift, or other means) can help in matching variations in assets to variations in income. In some countries, filers are also required to provide information on the source of financing for purchasing an asset. Some forms also require filers to include the cost of restoration or renovation. This is significant because the proceeds of corruption could potentially fund the transformation of a modest house into a mansion.

Although this information can provide a more comprehensive picture of filers' assets, it is also important to consider local context. Appropriate thresholds (reflecting substantive expenditures) and local practices in terms of justification documents (receipts, invoices, and the like) can also be useful. (For a summary, see figure 3.7).

FIGURE 3.7   Asset Acquisition

How, when, and where was asset acquired?

- Domestic vs. foreign assets
- Date of acquisition
- Mode of acquisition (for example, purchase vs. inheritance)
- Source of funding for acquisition

What Is the Nature of Ownership?

Some disclosure systems ask filers to indicate what part or percentage of an asset they own (for example, whether the filer owns an apartment wholly or 50 percent of it). Other systems also ask filers to disclose assets that they use but do not own, such as houses or vehicles (see figure 3.8).

What is the
nature of
ownership?

- % of ownership of asset
- Use vs. ownership

Declaring Income

Income is another category of information that is very widespread in financial disclosures, as it is relevant regardless of the objective of the system. It is key to identifying, preventing, and managing conflicts of interest, as well as to monitoring unjustified variations in wealth. The bases for approaching identification of income are three: *sources* (name of the legal entity or person from whom income is received, location of the entity, and company registration number), *types* (salaries, premiums, royalties, incomes from economic and commercial activities, incomes from selling movable and immovable assets, dividends, winnings from gambling, and inheritances), and *values* (amount, currency, per month or per year, gross, and/or net).

In systems that focus on identifying unjustified variations of wealth, capturing a snapshot of all the sources and values of income can be particularly useful. Fluctuations of income can be tracked across years in order to identify significant variations that could raise "red flags" in terms of illicit enrichment. Moreover, income fluctuations constitute an important component in comparing variations in assets with variations in income. Types of income can be an important complement to exact sources of income, as they indicate the nature of the activity that generated the income. For example, if only the name of a legal entity and an associated monetary value appeared on a form, it would be challenging to determine whether the income came from rent, dividends, a lucky casino day, or consultancy fees.

> There are three bases for approaching identification of income: sources, types, and values.

This information is also relevant for managing potential conflicts of interest and for identifying actual conflicts. For example, information provided about sources of income (such as the name of the legal entity or individual, the location of the entity, or the company registration number) as well as types of income could indicate a conflict of interest. An example of a conflict of interest would be an official receiving income from a company that was awarded contracts by the institution at which that official works.

Despite the usefulness of these categories of information, in some countries the only information required is the type of income (wages, income from securities, income from artistic activities, and so on) and the associated total value for that category (all wages and all income from securities), not the name of the legal entity or person from whom the income is received. In other countries, only some sources of income need to be declared. Both of these situations are problematic, regardless of the objective of the system.

As with many other categories of information in the form, details are important. For example, filers should be able to see on the form whether to include the gross value or the net value of their incomes. Indicating the relevant currency can also help, especially when different currencies are used for different sources of income.

If verification of the content of financial disclosures is a priority, information on income should appear in a manner that is consistent with information collected by other institutions, such as the tax administration, rather than create new categories. In some cases, the categories of income on the disclosure form did not match the breakdown in the tax return.

Declaring Securities

In the vast majority of financial disclosure systems, disclosing information on securities is a priority, even if not all systems adopt the same emphasis. Some focus on the issuer of the security or the nature of the security, some on the value of the security, and others on both aspects.

Some of the challenges that have been discussed with regard to expressing the values of immovable and movable assets are also relevant to securities, as the market value of securities is also in continuous flux. To manage this challenge, some systems ask filers to attach to their disclosure form a recent statement about the performance of their financial investments.

Some of the categories of information that are required in relation to securities include value (purchase and/or market), number of shares, unit price of shares, name of the entity in which the security is held, and other identifying information such as address (including country) and total percentage of shares owned in a company.

Many financial disclosure forms require filers to include information under a broad umbrella and provide a few examples of types of securities that should be included. In some countries, information is required under multiple well-defined categories, such as bonds or securities issued by a foreign government, municipal government bonds, futures, stock options, and corporate bonds. As expected, systems that focus on conflicts of interest request disaggregated information, with a focus on entities. In those systems that focus on illicit enrichment, however, broad umbrella categories are more common, with a focus on values.

> Given the variety of securities currently available, detailed guidance is needed.

Although use of securities information is quite widespread, it receives relatively less attention than other information when it comes to both improving the quality of the form and using the information collected. Given the variety of securities available, it comes as a surprise to see how little detailed guidance about the type of information that should be included is provided to filers, either on the form or in other instruments such as guidelines on filling out the form.

Declaring Business Relationships with Financial Institutions (Bank Accounts)

With regard to bank accounts, seven categories of information are typically included in the disclosure:

- Name of the financial institution
- Name of the account holder
- Bank account location (domestic or foreign)
- Bank account number
- Account type
- Balance in each account and the corresponding currency
- Interest accrued.

In some cases, filers are also required to explain the source of funds found in a bank account or to specify the year when the bank account was opened.

This is one category of information that does not raise any particular issues in terms of how the information is requested from the filer. The challenges appear when the information declared needs to be cross-checked, as bank secrecy laws may apply.

Declaring Liabilities

Common examples in forms include debts, obligations, loans, mortgages, guarantees, and cosignatures. The information that is typically required is the name of the creditor (either an individual or a legal entity), the date the filer incurred the liability, the repayment deadline, and the value.

Some forms also ask the filer to provide information on the terms of repayment and the purpose or reasons for which the liability was incurred, as well as on the amount of the principal and interest paid during a disclosure period. Some forms refer both to what the filer owes and to what is owed to the filer. In some cases, there is insufficient clarity on whether filers need to disclose both what they owe and what is owed to them.

Declaring Cash

This information is more commonly requested in countries that have cash-based economies. However, this category of information is particularly hard to deal with, given the difficulties of

- Proving existence
- Identifying the source

- Specifying the location
- Determining the appropriate threshold.

For example, in one disclosure system, filers must declare if they hold cash valued at more than US$2,400, and the currency in which it is held. The question that some practitioners raise is, what is the usefulness of this information? In most cases, the tools of a financial disclosure entity could not help confirm whether the value of cash disclosed by a filer is what he or she indeed held (for example, the amount could have been inflated with the expectation of justifying future gains from irregular sources). However, this information can be useful in the context of a broader corruption investigation. The disclosure of cash is a good example of a category of information that might not be useful for systematic or routine verification of financial disclosure, or for ongoing prevention and management of conflicts of interest; however, it can constitute a piece of the puzzle in a corruption investigation. As we will discuss at greater length in the chapter on accessing the information in financial disclosures, the information collected is relevant for more than just disclosure agencies.

Declaring Interests

Interests can comprise a variety of activities in which a filer is involved, aside from his or her main position in public office. These activities could be high-level positions, such as a member of a board of directors; other positions held in the public or private sector, such as a professor at a university, a consultant for a company, or involvement in a charity (for example, as a board member); and pretenure and posttenure activities, or those activities undertaken before taking office and those that the official may already know that he or she will perform after leaving office.

An important consideration in declaring interests is differentiating between pecuniary and nonpecuniary interests. Pecuniary interests entail money or can be valued in monetary terms; these include, for example, remunerated employment, and occupations other than the official position. Pecuniary interests can also include debts, assumed guarantees, insurance arrangements, pension schemes, and the like.

Nonpecuniary interests are not associated with financial gains. Such interests usually are memberships or unremunerated positions—for example, board functions in political parties, foundations, or charities, and volunteer work. Because the list of interests can be extensive, it is important to focus on those interests that in a given country may represent a high risk for conflicts of interest or even corruption.

Declaring Gifts

The disclosure of gifts is fairly limited when compared with other categories of information; however, it is still quite widespread. We use the term *gift* here as it is used by a number of disclosure systems; that is, it describes gifts beyond material goods (such as cell phones). We use it either as an umbrella term or as the first component of an enumeration that also includes nonmaterial gifts, services that were provided for free or at a discounted price, scholarships, grants, and so on. From our discussions with practitioners, the main concern is how to balance the risks that gifts pose in terms of integrity with the reality that gift-giving is a routine and important social practice in many cultures.

One approach is to exclude any gifts from close relatives, such as parents and children. These gifts might appear anyway under other headings, such as the source of financing for real estate or vehicles. Another approach is to set thresholds for the value of individual gifts; the official is required to disclose gifts that are at or above the threshold. In some countries, filers must disclose only those gifts that are received during the year from a single person or entity and that are worth more than a set monetary value. One specific area that raises concern among practitioners is how to approach gifts given at weddings, baptisms, and similar events. In some cultures, such gifts may translate into large amounts of cash.

Beneficial Ownership

The vast majority of financial disclosure systems require filers to provide information only on assets that they or their family members own directly (that is, to which they hold legal title). This means, for example, that filers must declare the shares that they own directly but do not need to disclose shares owned by a legal entity or arrangement (for example, a trust, a foundation, or a company) that they ultimately control. As a result, relevant information

> Including beneficial ownership in the declaration form makes it harder for public officials to distance themselves from what they truly own.

may be omitted from the disclosure form without the filer's having made a misrepresentation (box 3.1). Such a situation is not just a theoretical example but a reality often cited by practitioners, which makes the concept of beneficial ownership particularly relevant. Not including information on assets whose ultimate owners are public officials represents an important gap in the vast majority of financial disclosure systems, and it allows corrupt public officials to hide their assets from scrutiny. The recent heightened interest in beneficial ownership (by the Financial Action Task Force [FATF] and the Group of Twenty) makes this topic particularly relevant.[2]

But what would including beneficial ownership mean in practice? It would mean disclosure requirements going a step further, mandating that public officials declare not only what they legally own but also all of those assets that—despite being in the name of a third party, a trust, a foundation, or a company—are actually used or controlled by them.[3] The essence of beneficial ownership is not "ownership" in the ordinary sense of the word, but rather control and use; the legal ownership—holding a title to an asset—is irrelevant.

A few countries have implemented disclosure requirements that go beyond what is owned solely in the names of the filers or their family members. In one example, high-level and high-risk filers must disclose information about assets owned by a third party

BOX 3.1	Keeping the Truth (and Luxury New York Apartments) Hidden, while Not Lying

What do two former governors from Latin America, two children of public officials from East Asia, and a former member of parliament from an Eastern European country have in common? First and most obviously, they all were high-level public officials or closely related to them. Second, according to a recent investigation in the *New York Times* they all possess luxury real estate in New York and took several steps to hide their identity as the real owners of the properties.

Some of these steps involved buying condos through trusts, limited liability companies, or other entities that shielded their names. Such tactics made it very hard to identify the beneficial owner, to figure out who owned what, or who was the ultimate controller of a company (or other legal entity), since the names were not shown in the company records.

The *New York Times* investigation highlighted the fundamental, but often disregarded issue of declaring beneficial ownership in a public official's financial disclosures. Financial disclosure laws usually require high-level public officials to periodically declare their assets, income, and liabilities. In more than 90 percent of declaration forms, officials are required to declare their real estate holdings and those of their spouse and dependents. However, in most countries, if the public officials—like those described in the article—submit a declaration, they are **not** lying if they exclude their apartments. Financial disclosure requirements **do not** require them to declare assets owned through legal entities. In addition, although more than 80 percent of disclosure systems mandate that officials declare the shares they hold, officials do not have to declare shares if they are held in the name of a lawyer who holds them for the official's benefit.

Most high-level public officials are not corrupt. However, those who do engage in corrupt activities are likely to use entities such as companies, foundations, and trusts to hide their ill-gotten wealth. These conclusions are also confirmed by a recent **Transparency International UK report**. It showed that 75 percent of properties in the United Kingdom, under criminal investigation since 2004—as the suspected proceeds of corruption—made use of offshore corporate secrecy to hide the owners' identities. This in turn demands a lot of creativity, resources, and international cooperation from the prosecutors and investigators trying to detect some of these assets.

This explains why the *New York Times* took "more than a year to unravel the ownership of shell companies with condos in the Time Warner Center, by searching business and court records from more than 20 countries" (Story and Saul 2015). Journalists also interviewed dozens of people, examined hundreds of property records, and investigated the connections between lawyers or relatives named on deeds and the actual buyers. This was just to figure out the owners of apartments in **one** luxury building in Manhattan. Unfortunately, the expertise and resources available to practitioners in developing countries trying to trace similar types of assets are very meager relative to the challenge they face.

(continued next page)

Financial disclosures by public officials could be a useful tool in these kinds of investigations. Even though they are not the magic bullet for catching a corrupt official, especially those using sophisticated methods to hide their wealth, once there is an ongoing investigation, the information declared can be very helpful as evidence, in what has been both included and omitted. Furthermore, they can help catch a dishonest public official whose lavish lifestyle, including real estate in a prized location, could not be supported by the resources, such as a public sector salary, indicated in the declaration.

Incorporating the concept of beneficial ownership can increase the value of financial disclosures in the field of disclosure and beyond. It can help corruption investigations, assist the financial sector when undertaking due diligence of politically exposed persons (PEPs), and support civil society involved in ensuring the integrity of public officials. This is why, in recent years, we have suggested that beneficial ownership be included in declaration forms. How? Not only by requesting that public officials declare the assets they own in their name, but also those from which they benefit, even if there is no direct ownership, or additional assets over which they exercise control. Corrupt officials are increasingly using complex methods to try to hide their ill-gotten wealth. Disclosures, as a tool in the prevention of and fight against corruption, need to keep up and make it harder for corrupt officials to distance themselves from assets they truly own.

if the filer (or the filer's family members) either receives or has the right to receive income from an asset, or can directly or indirectly (through another natural or legal person) dispose of the asset.

In another country, officials must disclose trusts established for their or their family members' benefit, as well as trusts in which they serve as trustees. In this case, the information to be reported includes the name of the trust(s), the assets held in the trust, the value of the assets, and the income derived from the assets in the trust.

Some countries go beyond ownership of assets and refer to the "right of usufruct" or "use." However, the concept of "use" does not extend beyond movable and immovable assets. So, for example, it does not cover intangible assets, which means that some assets remain hidden.

Two of the issues in addressing beneficial ownership in a comprehensive manner are as follows: (a) filing populations are large and include a substantial proportion of low-level and mid-level officials for whom the term *beneficial ownership* is completely unfamiliar and, most likely, irrelevant; and (b) among financial disclosure practitioners, there is limited familiarity with beneficial ownership terminology.

One option for including the concept of beneficial ownership in financial disclosures is using or making reference to the definition of "beneficial owner" from the anti-money-laundering legislation. Nevertheless, low-level and mid-level officials who must declare still need to receive some very detailed guidance and advice on what the term means. Even if the term is irrelevant to them, officials still need to understand what the form says. This issue could also be dealt with by creating different disclosure forms or completion requirements for high-level and high-risk filers and for other categories of filers (as in the first country example in this section).

The limited familiarity with the concept of beneficial ownership among financial disclosure practitioners makes it hard for them to provide guidance to others and effectively monitor the implementation of new provisions and requirements on beneficial ownership. One practical way to work toward overcoming this obstacle could be to have financial intelligence units, other domestic and international practitioners, civil society, and AML/CFT (anti-money-laundering and combating the financing of terrorism) experts raise awareness among disclosure practitioners of beneficial ownership—both under the framework of national legislation and in practice. The next step would be for practitioners to draft guidance to filers that provides examples on how one might beneficially own real estate, other movables, or certain rights (such as licenses).

Despite the difficulties, it is worth considering adding beneficial ownership to the disclosure form, as that will make it harder for public officials to distance themselves from what they truly own.

Chapter 3—Key Recommendations

- The disclosure form itself is crucial in implementing what to declare.

- A strong form must be clear and comprehensive: it should collect relevant information in a user-friendly manner.

- Though the specific categories of information requested may vary a lot from one jurisdiction to another, the type of information collected by a given disclosure form should always be targeted to the objectives, corruption risks, and context of the financial disclosure system.

- Although requesting too much information complicates and weakens a form, personal identification information such as position, date of birth, and ID number should be as comprehensive as possible.

- The disclosure form should capture the most important elements of immovable and movable assets, such as the following: how to identify the asset; how to express the value of the asset; how, when, and where the asset was acquired; and what the nature of ownership is.

(continued next page)

Chapter 3—Key Recommendations *(continued)*

- Disclosing income is important for all disclosure systems. Depending on the goals of the system, disclosure of income should focus on source, type, and/or value.

- Forms should also mandate disclosure of stocks and securities, business relationships with financial institutions (bank accounts), liabilities, gifts, cash, and interests outside of public office, depending on the priorities of the system.

- Beneficial ownership should be included on the form, as it makes it harder for public officials to hide what they really own without having to lie about doing so.

- Finally, a user-friendly form should be designed for its target population. Users should face no guesswork or uncertainty when filling out the form.

Notes

1. Romania's website for disclosures can be accessed at http://declaratii.integritate.eu/home/navigare/cautare-avansata.aspx.
2. For more information, please see https://star.worldbank.org/star/about-us/g20-anti-corruption-working-group.
3. The internationally accepted definition of beneficial ownership is the one provided in the FATF recommendations; it defines the beneficial owner as the natural person(s) who ultimately owns or controls a legal person or legal arrangement. It is important to keep in mind that this definition was drafted for financial institutions or other service providers that, under AML/CFT (anti-money-laundering and combating the financing of terrorism) regulations, must fulfill certain obligations when dealing with a potential customer. One of these obligations is to establish the identity of the potential client's beneficial owner. For more information, refer to van der Does de Willebois and others (2011), 17–20.

References

Story, L., and S. Saul. 2015. "Stream of Foreign Wealth Flows to Elite New York Real Estate." *New York Times*, February 7. http://www.nytimes.com/2015/02/08/nyregion/stream-of-foreign-wealth-flows-to-time-warner-condos.html?_r=0.
van der Does de Willebois, E., E. M. Halter, R. A. Harrison, J. W. Park, and J. C. Sharman. 2011. *The Puppet Masters: How the Corrupt Use Legal Structures to Hide Stolen Assets and What to Do about It.* Washington, DC: World Bank.

4. The Submission Process

A public official in a remote area mentioned that she had to travel for several hours to reach the office where she could submit her disclosure. In another country, high-level public officials would use their official car and driver to get to the capital to submit their disclosures at the country's financial disclosure agency, as the law required them to do so in person. This implied taking the day off from regular duties, and the cost associated was high when considering all the travel expenses involved. In other countries, submitting the form may take only a couple of clicks on a computer.

The submission process, much like the form itself, represents a point of contact between the filer and the financial disclosure agency through which financial disclosure information flows. Indeed, if the form is the disclosure vehicle, then the submission process is the bridge between the filer and the agency.

It is important to note that *submission process* is a broad term that requires some further explanation. The term may refer to the physical transfer of the disclosure form from the filer to the agency. However, for the transfer to occur successfully, other elements—such as preliminary checking of information received, data management and transfer, communication with filers, and more—must also align. As such, submission not only occupies a large part of the financial disclosure conversation, but also has significant implications for the effectiveness and functionality of the disclosure system as a whole.

> The submission process represents the starting point, and its flaws will inevitably trickle down to the rest of the system.

In the majority of cases, the submission process poses significant challenges to disclosure systems, both new and old. Most of our work ultimately involves issues with the submission process, even if the initial inquiry does not. The submission process is a vital element of and is intrinsically linked to all of the other elements of the disclosure system. It represents the starting point, and any flaws will inevitably affect the rest of the system. Therefore one cannot design an effective submission process without considering the other parts of the disclosure system, and conversely, one cannot design an effective disclosure system without paying close attention to the submission process.

Many factors feed into the design of an effective submission process, such as the size and composition of the filing population and the expertise and technological capacity of the agency. Ultimately, a system must be uniquely tailored to the country. Therefore, those who are designing and implementing a system need to look at their objectives, context, and limitations. In all cases, creativity and resourcefulness are extremely important at this stage of the disclosure process. This chapter highlights the latest trends in the streamlining of submission processes and also provides insight on how to overcome some common submission challenges, with the aim of providing guidance for achieving a country's own best process.

Key Elements of the Submission Process

Every functional submission process includes several basic elements. Although the elements are nearly always the same, how they are implemented can vary significantly. These common elements work in concert to enable the flow of information between filers, the agency, and, often, the public:

- Creating and managing a list of filers
- Communicating with the filer both about the duty to submit a disclosure and about assistance with the filing steps
- Completing the disclosure form and submitting it to the appropriate body
- Performing quality control or a review of the disclosure for completeness, internal consistency, and obvious filing errors
- Storing and managing the submitted data
- Analyzing and reporting results of the submission process.

As illustrated in figure 4.1, the submission process is dynamic and requires each element to feed into the next one and to be based on the previous one. Although we

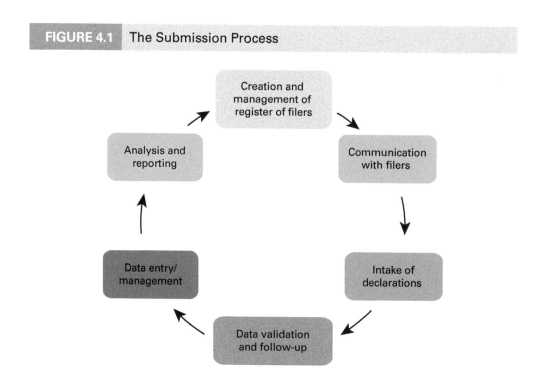

FIGURE 4.1 The Submission Process

discuss each element individually, it is important to note that the effectiveness of the submission process and the resulting submission compliance rate depend on the system working well as a whole.

The Register of Filers

The foundation of the submission process is the register of filers. Therefore, key questions must be addressed in a way that reflects the disclosure requirements and the capacity of a given system: How is the list of filers created? Who manages the list? How is it kept up to date?

Keeping track of the *number* and *identities* of officials who are required to file is typically done in coordination with human resources (HR) administration offices in the government agencies or entities in which public officials are employed. Establishing communication and coordination mechanisms with HR offices is thus a vital step in ensuring that the registry of filers is accurate and up to date. We have seen this done in several ways, from having the HR office provide an updated list (as illustrated in figure 4.2), to seamlessly importing data about the filers directly from the centralized payroll system.

Building a list of actual filers can be quite challenging. Sometimes it may be unrealistic to try to build a centralized one. Indeed, approximately 65 percent of the surveyed

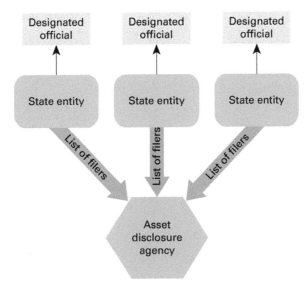

FIGURE 4.2 Country Example: Creating and Maintaining a List of Filers

Note: In this system, the designated official in each state entity (a) draws up a list of filers that is based on categories of officials defined by law, (b) notifies the filers of their obligation to file, (c) submits the list of filers to the financial disclosure agency, (d) assists filers in submitting disclosures (online), (e) forwards the hardcopy (paper) disclosures to the Office of the Inspector General, and (f) updates lists of filers.

FIGURE 4.3   Preferred Methods for Checking Compliance

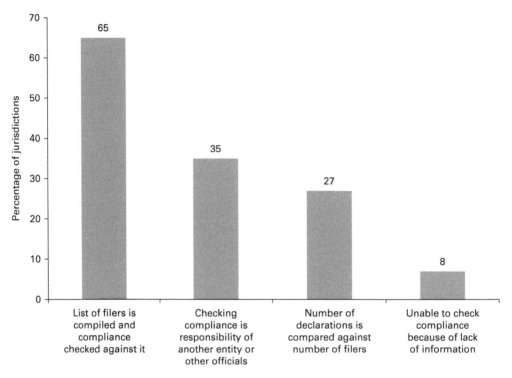

Note: Approximate percentages based on the analysis of 52 disclosure jurisdictions.

jurisdictions maintain a register of filers (see figure 4.3). Some of the challenges that may arise when trying to draw up that list are (a) absence of a legal obligation for HR officers to support the disclosure system, (b) lack of centralized personnel information for the public sector, (c) lack of up-to-date personnel information, (d) poor communication between financial disclosure officials and HR officials, and (e) lack of resources for HR offices to gather up-to-date data. (For a more in-depth discussion about the register of filers, see chapter 2).

Communication with the Filer

Establishing communication between filers and the disclosure agency is a vital step in ensuring submission compliance. In general, an agency needs to communicate with filers to (a) inform them of their obligation to file as well as of the filing requirements and deadlines, and (b) provide additional support. More specifically, communication with filers should include the following information:

- The purpose of the disclosure requirement
- The filer's obligations (how often he or she needs to file, deadlines, procedures, and so forth)

FIGURE 4.4 Country Example: Communication with Filers

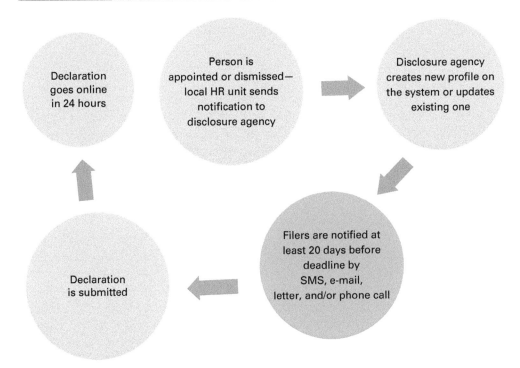

Source: Based on the financial disclosure system in Georgia.
Note: HR = human resources. The example highlights changes to the existing master list of filers.

- The procedures for review and investigation (when relevant)
- The types of sanctions and procedures for enforcement (when relevant)
- Potential conflicts of interest and how to prevent an actual conflict from arising (where applicable).

Whether communicating the obligation to file or providing support, this is an excellent opportunity for the agency to be creative and resourceful. Being mindful of the resources available, the capacity of the filers, and the disclosure requirements, agencies can employ a vast array of methods to reach out to and respond to filers. For example, in one country, the disclosure agency not only sends e-mail messages to filers—including a calendar with key dates and venues where the agency will provide face-to-face support to filers—but also provides on the agency website the form, guidelines for filling out the form, and a video on how to submit the form (see figure 4.4.). Multiple communication channels may be used to meet the same objective and to adjust the methods to meet the needs of both the filers and the agency.

Obligation to Disclose

Depending on the structure of the system, either the disclosure agency or another office—such as the HR office within the filer's agency—bears responsibility for notifying officials of their obligation to submit a disclosure, be it upon appointment, dismissal, or promotion, or annually. This can be done using a variety of channels, including informative posters on bulletin boards, phone calls, mail, e-mail, radio announcements, and even text messages. Figure 4.4 illustrates how this element fits into the submission process in a sample country.

Support for Filers

It is imperative that there is a strong support mechanism for filers. Some examples of common communication tools are websites, the media, designated staff, telephone hot-lines, detailed guidelines, and answers to frequently asked questions (FAQs) attached to blank forms. Other support systems include online chat services and a resident ombuds-man or ethics officer assigned to provide support directly to filers on potential conflicts of interest.

Increasingly, countries are also developing detailed guides on how to fill out disclo-sure forms. These guides can make the process of filing much easier and less time consuming for the filer and greatly increase the quality of the information collected. For example, it is useful for the filer to know that, if he or she owns the land beneath a house, then that land also needs to be declared under the land category. When it comes to declaring income, guidance on the precise entries in the tax return that should be included makes the filing easier. Declaring information on trusts, such as investments held by a trust or income received from a trust, is made easier through the detailed information in a guide. These instruments can include examples of how information should be declared. Such guides are also living documents that agencies can update regularly on the basis of common errors they see and questions they receive from filers. In systems that use electronic filing (e-filing), the information in the guides can be delivered in an even more user-friendly way by being embedded into the e-filing form.

In countries that have a conflict of interest dimen-sion to their financial disclosure system, communi-cation and support tools and processes are of vital importance. Too often, greater focus is placed on sanctions for failure to disclose interests and actual conflicts of interest, and insufficient attention is given to creating guidance tools or providing in-person advisory services to support the process.

> Communication makes the process of filing much eas-ier and less time consum-ing for the filer and greatly increases the quality of the information collected.

Communication with filers and the public plays another significant role in the submis-sion process. It is an opportunity for the agency to highlight the importance of filing, raise awareness of the disclosure system among filers and the general public, and rein-force a culture of integrity. Again, disclosure agencies should be creative and should employ whatever channels they might have at their disposal to accomplish these goals. For instance, using notices in hallways, radio announcements, or television spots can raise awareness levels and, ultimately, compliance rates.

Completing and Submitting the Form

This step is fairly straightforward: the filer fills in the form. What varies here is (a) how the filer receives the form and (b) how he or she goes about completing and submitting it. Generally, this process is done in one way or a combination of ways (figure 4.5):

- **Paper:** The filer either picks up or receives by mail or from a financial disclosure official a hard copy of the form. The filer then fills in the hard copy and either mails or delivers the signed form to the appropriate authority.
- **Download:** The filer accesses and downloads the form from the agency's website. The filer then prints, completes, and mails or delivers the hard copy to the appropriate authority.
- **Web form:** The filer accesses the form online. The filer then completes the form—either on or offline—prints it, and mails or delivers the hard copy to the appropriate authority.
- **Web form with online submission:** The filer accesses the form online. The filer then completes the form on or offline and submits the completed form online.

When deciding which methods to use, agencies must consider how the methods will work in their context and what consequences might arise from choosing one method over another. Figure 4.6 shows that, in almost 70 percent of the disclosure systems we analyzed, filers submit forms *in person* at the office of the disclosure agency. This requirement may have significant and often unforeseen repercussions. For instance, in one country, high-ranking officials who lived outside the capital but who could submit disclosures only in person at the disclosure agency used their service cars when

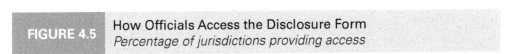

FIGURE 4.5 How Officials Access the Disclosure Form
Percentage of jurisdictions providing access

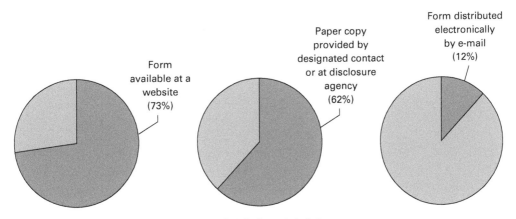

Form available at a website (73%)

Paper copy provided by designated contact or at disclosure agency (62%)

Form distributed electronically by e-mail (12%)

Note: Approximate percentages based on analysis of 52 disclosure jurisdictions.

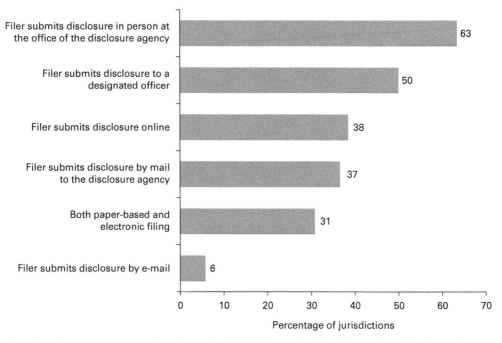

FIGURE 4.6 Methods for Submitting Disclosure Forms

Filer submits disclosure in person at the office of the disclosure agency — 63

Filer submits disclosure to a designated officer — 50

Filer submits disclosure online — 38

Filer submits disclosure by mail to the disclosure agency — 37

Both paper-based and electronic filing — 31

Filer submits disclosure by e-mail — 6

Percentage of jurisdictions

Note: Approximate percentages based on the analysis of 52 disclosure jurisdictions. The numbers reflect the fact that systems often employ more than one method of submission.

complying with their obligation to disclose. This essentially amounted to subsidized vacations to the capital for those officials. There are also many examples in which hundreds or thousands of officials have stood in line under the sun or in heavy rain on the last day before the yearly submission deadline. These situations almost always cause logistical nightmares that provoke discontent among filers and tarnish the reputation of the disclosure process and the institutions managing it.

In a substantial number of systems, filers can submit disclosures both online and on paper. Although some filers take advantage of the e-filing option, others do not. This is attributable to, among other causes, limited access to or lack of familiarity with technology, mistrust in electronic submission process, and the fact that not all filers have digital signatures.[1] To create predictability in the administration of the submission process, one option is to allow both types of submission to coexist for a transitional period before ultimately eliminating the paper-based system.

Details of the submission process—not just the overall design—matter. For example, if it is decided that the form is to be filled out on hard copy (that is, either picked up or printed out), must it be typed or can it be handwritten? Managing and carrying out basic analysis of data from handwritten forms can be particularly challenging, even when processing only a few disclosures. However, if filers do not have access to computers, completing the forms by hand might be the only choice. We are seeing fewer and fewer cases in which high-level and high-risk officials do not have access to computers at their workplace. We have also seen numerous occasions when, given the choice between completing the form online (or typing in the answers) and filling out a hard copy by hand, filers choose the latter. Figure 4.7 shows that, although other options exist, the majority of filers still fill out forms by hand (69 percent). A related question is whether the form needs to be notarized. If it does, how easy is it for filers to do so? Are additional costs involved? These are the types of questions and considerations that must be taken into account when designing the submission procedures. Looking to other systems for examples of methods is useful, but the choice ultimately comes down to what works best in the environment given subsequent constraints and consequences.

There is quite a bit of range in the institutional design of the submission process. This range is due, in part, to differences in the underlying objectives of disclosure systems as a whole, but is also a result of the political and institutional environments in which they exist. A country might opt to have each filer submit a completed form directly to the disclosure agency (or relevant body). We often see this in countries that have smaller filing populations. For instance, in a country that has fewer than 5,000 filers, this type of system might work. However, in a system that has, say, 50,000 filers, direct submission to the agency may not be the best choice. Indeed, in that situation, one approach is for filers to submit forms to designated officers within their own agencies who then transfer the completed forms to the central disclosure agency. This is an example of a decentralized system (see figure 4.2). Some countries opt to create a hybrid of centralized and decentralized systems by having some officials, perhaps high-level or designated high-risk officials, submit directly to the central agency while the remaining disclosures are submitted to HR officers.[2]

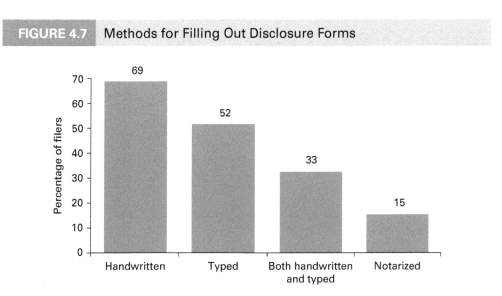

FIGURE 4.7   Methods for Filling Out Disclosure Forms

Note: Approximate percentages based on analysis of 52 disclosure jurisdictions.

Ensuring Compliance and Quality Control

As described earlier, achieving submission compliance is the result of multiple steps working in tandem. As illustrated in figure 4.8, the path to compliance is a dialogue between the filer and the agency, with information flowing back and forth throughout the process.

Submission compliance is a common indicator used for measuring the effectiveness of a financial disclosure system. It is primarily based on timely completion and submission of the disclosure form. Indeed, most statistics look at the compliance rate in terms of the number of completed or submitted forms relative to the number of required forms. For example, a country might have a 90 percent compliance rate, on the basis of the fact that 90 percent of required filers filed a completed form on time. However, this number is only one half of the compliance equation.

In our view, the accuracy and completeness of submitted forms is as important an indicator as is the percentage of filers who submit their forms. Inaccurate or unreliable forms have little value. In one country, a disclosure form contained information on a house with 3,854 rooms—and yet this disclosure counted as a completed disclosure form and contributed to the country's high compliance rate. In another country, the financial intelligence unit determined that all 50 forms reviewed during analytical work contained inaccurate data.

A check of accuracy and completeness is not a matter of verification, but rather a cursory check of the data. This check does not mean that the information has been verified,

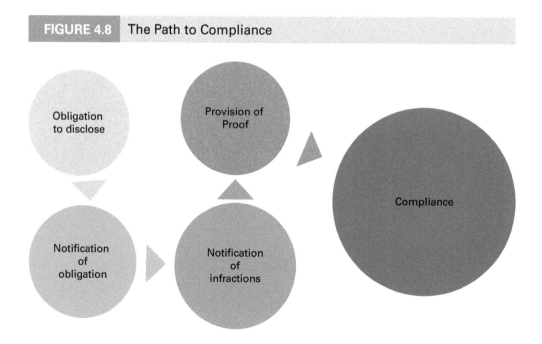

FIGURE 4.8 The Path to Compliance

but rather that it prima facie makes sense. It is imperative that this check be a part of every system, especially when an agency is considering using an automated verification system down the road. Ensuring the submission of "clean" or quality data at this stage of the financial disclosure process ultimately allows for more efficient and effective verification. The accuracy and completeness of forms should therefore be a contributing factor in assessing a system's submission compliance levels.

Therefore, rather than focusing solely on submission compliance, a better measure of success is the achievement of an optimal submission process. This requires both high levels of compliance *and* high levels of data quality (figure 4.9). It is only when both of these elements are present that a disclosure system can truly function as a tool for accountability and transparency. That said, countries might not be able to achieve "optimal submission" immediately, nor be able to focus on improving both compliance and data quality simultaneously. In such cases, focusing on increasing compliance or quality independently may work, as long as both are eventually addressed.

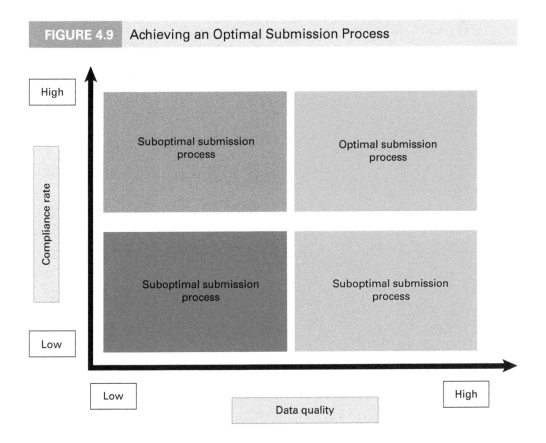

FIGURE 4.9 Achieving an Optimal Submission Process

Data Collection and Management

At this point, most disclosure systems, whether partially automated or not, will perform some form of data transfer from the disclosure forms to a database to enable administrative functions associated with data retrieval, verification procedures, data tracking, and—where applicable—publication of data online or in other media for public access. In an increasing number of systems, information from forms filed electronically is automatically transferred to a database. In many systems, the information from paper disclosures is still transcribed into a data management software program. In looking toward implementing verification and perhaps even automated verification, it is important to note whether the database is searchable across data points. Although data management is an essential stage in the submission process, over 20 percent of the systems studied do not do any data entry or electronic archiving (figure 4.10).

Some very important questions arise at this stage of the submission process: How is the information organized in the database? Is it sorted by name, by ID number, or by another element? Is it organized by the same methods used by other databases in other agencies? It is useful at this stage to standardize the data collected and the design of the database. Ultimately, the goal of verifying the information using external databases, such as that of the tax administration or vehicle registries, will require a level of standardization of information and the existence of data that are common to both data sets.

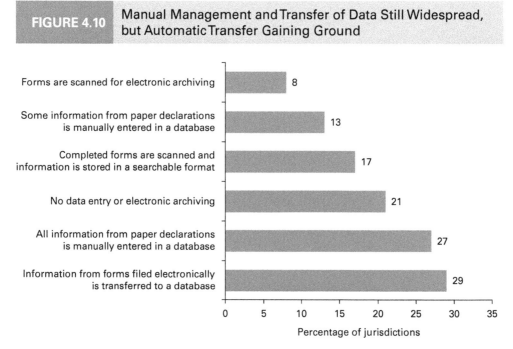

FIGURE 4.10 Manual Management and Transfer of Data Still Widespread, but Automatic Transfer Gaining Ground

Forms are scanned for electronic archiving — 8

Some information from paper declarations is manually entered in a database — 13

Completed forms are scanned and information is stored in a searchable format — 17

No data entry or electronic archiving — 21

All information from paper declarations is manually entered in a database — 27

Information from forms filed electronically is transferred to a database — 29

Percentage of jurisdictions

Note: Approximate percentages based on the analysis of 52 disclosure jurisdictions.

Analysis and Reporting

Analysis of both the compliance rates and the information provided in the disclosure can provide financial disclosure agencies with valuable information on the weak links in the disclosure process. For instance, an analysis of the compliance rates across agencies may reveal that one does not comply adequately with the filing requirements. Perhaps this is a failure of management in that agency, or a lack of communication or, perhaps, a red flag pointing to potential corrupt behavior that warrants further monitoring. The same holds for an analysis of the data provided in the disclosure forms. In some cases, frequent mistakes in the same category might indicate that either the form or the guidelines need more clarity.

Reporting on the performance of the disclosure system serves a different purpose. Sharing the compliance data, along with the system's mandate and procedures, may help enlist the public and civil society as partners in achieving the system's objectives and can increase the likelihood of public attention to unethical conduct or potential conflicts of interest. This public awareness and involvement may ultimately increase the agency's effective detection of violations through public complaints. To enlist the public effectively, however, the disclosure agency needs a mechanism to track and report the results of the disclosure process.

Effective reporting not only is important for engaging the public, but also helps inform (or remind) policy makers and legislators about the agency's mandate, the disclosure requirement, and the role that financial disclosure plays in establishing a culture of accountability and transparency. In countries where anticorruption mechanisms have been politicized, effective reporting may help offset fears of political bias, retaliation, or other dishonest motivations. It can also indicate the limits inherent in the disclosure system (for example, with regard to imposing and enforcing sanctions).

Electronic versus Paper-Based Submission

Currently, most disclosure systems are paper based or have limited electronic elements. However, systems are increasingly either transitioning to an electronic filing and management system or are contemplating making the transition. This is the area of greatest change now taking place in the world of financial disclosure.

In practice, many systems incorporate at least one electronic element. For example, in many systems, the blank disclosure form is available on the website of the disclosure agency, from which it can be downloaded and printed before being mailed to the disclosure agency or collected by an HR officer. In other systems, an electronic database of filers is regularly updated by HR offices or from payroll databases.

With regard to the management of the information collected, some systems (27 percent of the systems analyzed; see figure 4.10) transfer information from paper-based disclosures into an electronic database. Particularly in systems with a high number of filers, the manual transfer of data from paper disclosures to an electronic database is both unsustainable and

> Transitioning to electronic filing is the area of greatest change now taking place in the world of financial disclosure.

problematic for the analysis of the information. It is unsustainable because this type of data transfer requires significant resources. Moreover, a backlog frequently emerges because the resources that can be made available cannot match the volume of disclosures. It is also problematic for analysis of the data because human error is unavoidable.

Handwritten disclosures (used in 69 percent of systems analyzed; see figure 4.7) complicate the transfer of the information in disclosures to an electronic database, as well as automated analysis. To transfer the data, financial disclosure staff members must spend significant time deciphering handwriting on thousands of disclosures. Even where handwriting recognition software is available, financial disclosure staff members may still face the challenge of dealing with scanned or edited forms in various layouts and formats, thus slowing down the process.

Other systems (17 percent of the systems analyzed; see figure 4.10) scan disclosures both for internal processing and for public accessibility. The benefit of this approach is that the disclosures are systematized by the agency and searchable by both the agency staff and the general public. For example, disclosure agency staff members can easily retrieve the disclosures of a certain official or certain categories of officials, or create a folder for each official with disclosures submitted over the years. However, when the number of filers is high, the scanning can be very expensive and resource intensive. Also, scanned forms limit the capacity to perform data analysis and the usability of the data when they become public. Both when disclosures are scanned and when the data are manually transferred from financial disclosures into an electronic database, storage of paper disclosures remains a significant challenge.

As mentioned earlier, more and more systems are working toward developing electronic tools for filing and managing disclosures. Some are completely paperless, whereas others still include a paper-based component. In a small number of countries—a number that will likely increase—all disclosures are filed electronically without any option for filing a paper copy. In other countries, a small percentage of officials file electronically using digital signatures, whereas the majority of filers—who do not have a digital signature—file online and also print the disclosure filed electronically, sign it, and mail it to the disclosure agency.

Although all systems may ultimately transition to electronic filing and management, the question is, when is a system ready for this transition? In our experience, some systems are ready to make the transition in the near future, whereas for others the foundation for making the transition will take many years to build.

How can a disclosure agency decide on the timing of the transition? One key factor is whether filers can have access to the tools that would enable them to file electronically. For example, if Internet access is unreliable even in the capital, how can filers outside the capital be expected to file electronically? If some

> Although all systems may ultimately transition to an electronic filing and management system, the question is, when is a system ready for this transition?

filers do not have access to a computer or to the Internet in their offices, how can they be expected to comply with the obligation to disclose? Making the Internet available in all the government offices where filers work, or at least in the vicinity of the filers' offices, does not depend on the disclosure agency. Therefore, even if the e-filing tools can be created, the transition to e-filing sometimes may need to be postponed until other services become functional.

A good indicator of the right timing for the transition is whether other services, such as filing taxes, are done electronically. The availability of funds for building an e-filing system also plays a role. However, beyond the costs of software and hardware are other costs that might also need to be considered, such as the costs of making digital signatures[3] available to all filers or of training filers in using the new filing system.

Not being ready to make the transition to a full-fledged electronic filing and management system does not mean that a system is ineffective. In such cases, the size of the filing population is of the utmost importance, as is the adoption of a risk-based approach in the analysis of the information declared. A paper-based system also requires investing greater resources in organizing the logistics of collecting, storing, and organizing the disclosures.

Challenges in Transitioning to Electronic-Based Submission

Even in countries with good levels of Internet access for filers and information technology capacity, the transition from a paper-based to an electronic-based system is complex. A broad array of elements needs to come together for a successful transition. For example, in most countries, legislation needs to allow or specify that filing be carried out electronically. The use of a digital signature for the authentication of disclosures also requires a basis in law. In some countries, funds also need to be allocated from the national budget, not only for designing and maintaining the system but also for issuing digital signatures to the filers.

As in a paper-based system, one of the main building blocks of an electronic system is the registry of filers. Matching the positions of officials who are obliged to declare to the names of those holding the positions can be of even greater importance in an electronic system, as officials need to be given the tools to access the e-filing system and to authenticate the disclosure. In one country, each filer receives a letter with a username and password to gain access to the e-filing system. This means that the disclosure agency has a list of all the filers who need to submit disclosures and is able to contact them. What helps in the smooth implementation of this aspect of the e-filing system is that the total number of filers in this country is only about 3,000. Moreover, matching positions obliged to declare to actual names is facilitated by the fact that payroll information is centralized in this country and that HR officers have an obligation to notify the disclosure agency whenever an official with an obligation to declare is dismissed or appointed.

Reaching out to the filers with the sign-in information is much more complicated in countries that have tens of thousands or hundreds of thousands of filers, and that have either no centralized payroll or a limited role for HR officers in the functioning of the disclosure system. Even if the burden is placed on the filers to request the tools for signing into the system, such as digital signatures, the logistics of this process can be overwhelming. This is another example of how the size of the filing population affects the functioning of the disclosure system.

The simple ability of a filer to sign into the e-filing system, fill out a form, and submit it is not enough. Safeguards must be put in place to ensure that the person who filled out the disclosure and submitted it is indeed the official who has the obligation to file. This is particularly relevant if the information filed electronically is made publicly available. The ability of another person to file a disclosure in the name of a filer can seriously affect the credibility of the e-filing process. Moreover, if a form filed electronically is used as evidence, any weakness in the authentication process can be detrimental to the success of legal processes.

As with other electronic services that collect personal information, data security is of the utmost importance for an agency that uses e-filing. This issue is always raised by future users of e-filing systems. Data security is a priority not only in countries where public access to the content of the disclosure is limited, but in all systems that store and process disclosures. Moreover, the integrity of the information must be ensured, so that the content of disclosures cannot be changed by unauthorized persons.

Seeking the expertise and using the lessons learned from other institutions that have transitioned to e-filing can help agencies identify potential obstacles ahead of time and resolve them before they materialize. In one country, the representatives of the tax administration volunteered to share their experiences in order to help their colleagues in the disclosure agency avoid making the same mistakes that they made. Within a country, there may be other agencies with expertise in the design and implementation of e-services who can advise the financial disclosure agency. In one country, e-filing is being developed at the same time as several other e-services, thereby leveraging economies of scale from the standpoint of both finance and expertise.

In the transition to e-filing, both disclosure agencies and disclosure practitioners need to be deeply involved in the design of the terms of reference for the electronic system and in the subsequent development of the system. Information technology experts alone cannot be expected to design a template for an electronic disclosure form that best fits the needs of disclosure practitioners for data management and analysis.

Setting realistic timelines and deadlines for planning and making the transition is of the utmost significance. Setting a goal of making the transition over a short period of time allows for only limited time to pilot the e-filing system, identify and fix any glitches found, or seriously tackle data security issues. Time to inform filers about the new system and to organize training for them on the new e-filing processes also needs to be built in.

Chapter 4—Key Recommendations

- An effective financial disclosure system requires a *well-performing submission process*: submission is the starting point, and its flaws inevitably trickle down to the rest of the system.

- A functional submission process must have several *basic elements*:
  - A comprehensive *register of filers*
  - Effective *communication* between the filers and the disclosure agency
  - Processes for completion and submission *of disclosure forms*
  - *Quality control* or a review of the disclosures for completeness, internal consistency, or obvious filing errors
  - *Storage* and *management* of the submitted data
  - *Analysis* and *reporting*.

- The *list of filers* is recommended and should be used to keep track of the *identities* of officials who need to declare and to cross-check compliance.

- *Communication* with filers is key. It makes the submission process much easier and less time consuming for the filer and can greatly increase the quality of the information collected. Support tools—such as websites, media, designated staff, telephone hotlines, detailed guidelines, and answers to frequently asked questions attached to blank forms—have proven their effectiveness and should be employed where possible.

- The experiences of many countries show that the costs of collecting handwritten disclosures greatly outweigh the benefits. It is advisable to put more emphasis on typed disclosures and to reduce the instances in which disclosures have to be submitted in person at the office of the disclosure agency.

- To achieve an optimal submission process, the disclosure agency must both receive high-quality data and maintain a high compliance rate.

- Electronic filing and data management is highly recommended. Systems must base the timing of the transition to electronic-based filing and data management on variables such as Internet access, digital signatures, information technology capacity, and so forth.

- Successful *transitions to electronic filing* use lessons learned from launching other e-governance services, involve multiple stakeholders, and budget for ample preparation and testing time.

Notes

1. A digital signature (standard electronic signature) takes the concept of a traditional paper-based signature and turns it into an electronic "fingerprint." This fingerprint, or coded message, is unique to both the document and the signer, and binds the

two together. Digital signatures ensure the authenticity of the signer. Any changes made to the document after it has been signed invalidate the digital signature, thereby protecting against signature forgery and information tampering. By their very nature, digital signatures help organizations sustain signer authenticity, accountability, and data integrity, and help prevent the repudiation of signed electronic documents and forms. For more information, please see http://www.arx .com/learn/about-digital-signature/digital-signature-faq/.

2. For more information on this topic, please see StAR (2012), 28–32.

3. In some countries, there is a cost associated with the use of digital signatures in general (aside from its potential use for financial disclosure). Even if the cost is very low, filers should not be expected to cover this cost for financial disclosure purposes.

Reference

StAR (Stolen Asset Recovery Initiative). 2012. *Public Office, Private Interests: Accountability through Income and Asset Disclosure*. Washington, DC: World Bank.

5. Verification of Information

Each year, the financial disclosure agency in one country receives about 350,000 disclosures; in election years, the number is even higher. Most of them are submitted in paper format. Given the very high volume of disclosures, only a small number can be verified. The main triggers for verification are complaints from individuals and legal entities, and ex officio reasons (for example, on the basis of media reports). In the past five years, the financial disclosure agency has started the verification process in only a limited number of cases. However, this has not been without results. In more than 1,700 cases, the financial disclosure agency found significant differences between the acquired assets and income, conflicts of interest and incompatibility violations, and indications of criminal acts such as false statements or corruption.

Verification is the process by which the content of disclosures is reviewed to detect inconsistencies, red flags, potential conflicts of interest, and other problems. Before going into more detail on what this process entails, we need to clarify a point on terminology. Throughout this chapter and this guide we use the term *verification*. However, the process of verifying the content of financial disclosures is referred to by a myriad of terms: *analysis, monitoring, review, inspection, audit, checking,* and others. Moreover, verification can mean very different things, depending on the level and scope of the analysis. For instance, it could refer to a single-step process such as screening for internal consistencies in the information submitted by the filer; or it could refer to multiple steps that include checking for internal consistency for all disclosures, checking for variations across years, and even comparing the data with outside sources of information.

> Verification is the point in the financial disclosure process where the information or data collected can tell a story.

At a basic level, verification sends a strong message that reinforces the culture of integrity promoted through financial disclosure and that strengthens its deterrent effect. Through checking the content of disclosures, agencies can detect potential conflicts of interest, advise officials on how to manage their interests, and ultimately prevent actual conflicts of interest. In addition, if officials know that someone will look into the accuracy of their disclosures, they may think twice about engaging in corrupt or illicit activities.

Although such a preventive effect is vital to the overall effectiveness of the system, verification is also the point in the financial disclosure process where the information or data collected can "speak." Identifying filers, outlining what should be declared, and establishing how information is to be collected are all very important, but those steps do not reveal anything about how the system is working or where there might be

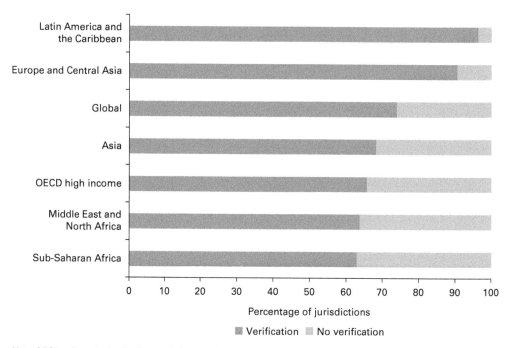

| FIGURE 5.1 | Verification of the Content of Financial Disclosures (by Law) Is Particularly Widespread in Latin American and the Caribbean and in Europe and Central Asia |

Percentage of jurisdictions

■ Verification ■ No verification

Note: OECD = Organisation for Economic Co-operation and Development. Approximate percentages based on the analysis of 153 jurisdictions.

corrupt activities. Checking the information and conducting some level of analysis are good ways to see what the data are showing. Verification is thus the process by which a deeper understanding of the data is obtained.

In general, countries recognize the importance of verification as an element of financial disclosure, with approximately 74 percent of jurisdictions including verification provisions in their legal framework for financial disclosure. In Latin America and the Caribbean and in Europe and Central Asia, the percentage of disclosure countries that have verification provisions is even higher: 96 percent in the former and 90 percent in the latter (see figure 5.1).

Objectives of Verification

The primary objective of the verification process is to ensure that all the information that was submitted by the filer is accurate. "Accurate" means that (a) the filer has omitted no required information, and (b) all information filed reflects reality (that is, no assets or interests are misrepresented). Incomplete or inaccurate information hinders the overall objective of the disclosure system.

Identifying acts of corruption is not the primary objective of verification. However, some filers deliberately omit information about their assets or income in their disclosures because they might represent proceeds of corruption, or they misrepresent their interests in the private sector in order to hide conflicts of interest. Thus, the verification process should be designed to identify inconsistencies, inaccurate data, and red flags, which can ultimately lead to the detection of the following:

- False statements (including both omitted information and over-disclosure of assets or income not held by the official)
- Unjustified variations of wealth
- Illicit enrichment
- Potential and actual conflicts of interest
- Incompatibilities between an official's mandate and other positions
- Information relevant for corruption/tax crime/money-laundering investigations.

We have yet to encounter a disclosure system that manages to carry out verification in order to detect all of the above. Some verification systems have as a sole objective the identification of actual or potential conflicts of interest. Others focus on a combination of identification of false statements, unjustified variations of wealth, conflict of interest situations, incompatibilities, and information relevant for corruption investigations.

In most cases, financial disclosure systems collect a unique mix of categories of information. This means that, although some information might also be disclosed in tax returns, the overall mix of information is unique to the financial disclosure system. For example, in some cases, a tax return would not capture information on liabilities; on bank accounts that do not generate income; or on movable assets such as livestock, paintings, and antiques. The analysis of all the information in financial disclosures can provide indications of unjustified wealth and triggers for corruption investigations that would not otherwise have come to the attention of the authorities.

Expectations about the results and impact of the verification process must be managed. This is primarily due to the numerous elements needed to enable a verification process to deliver substantial results. These elements may include a financial disclosure form that is designed to support the verification process; skilled staff members; some reliable registries or databases for cross-checking information; and sanctions that are proportional, enforceable, and visible. In many cases, getting all of these elements in place does not happen overnight. This is why, in many cases, a gradual approach to building a verification system is advisable.

Moreover, realistic expectations are necessary in situations where officials who engage in corrupt activities use entities such as companies, foundations, and trusts to hide their ill-gotten wealth.[1] For example, it can be very difficult to verify information on real estate held abroad when the asset is not registered in the name of the official, but rather he or she is the beneficiary or the person who can exercise control over the asset.[2] Even investigations that use mutual legal assistance may have difficulty identifying beneficial ownership.

It is important to be aware of all the tools and resources that contribute to an effective system, as well as to be realistic about what can be achieved. At the same time, building an effective verification system is possible for countries and institutions with considerable funding and staffing resources, as well as for those with fewer resources. Phasing in the verification process gradually, perhaps by adopting a risk-based approach or by prioritizing sources of information during the verification process, can help deliver results when resources are limited.

> Although verification is a powerful process, expectations about results and impact must be managed.

In designing the verification process, serious thought should be given to the desired function of verification as it relates to the larger system. For instance, is the objective of the financial disclosure system detection or deterrence? Is the goal to catch numerous minor infractions committed by public officials of varying rank or to catch one "big fish"? The answers to these questions will likely determine whether a system will conduct systematic and widespread verification or will focus on complaints and other ad hoc checks. Another question to consider is, what is the measure of success? For example, is the measure of success based on the quantity or the quality of cases prosecuted? Such larger objectives are also based on the specific resource and capacity restraints, as well as on available sanctions. Financial disclosure is not a linear process but rather a feedback loop, with each element influencing the other. Verification should thus fit into this feedback loop in both its design and its results.

Verification Methodology

Determining Which Disclosures to Verify

Many agencies and practitioners have difficulty identifying which disclosures they should focus on for verification. If it were feasible, most practitioners would like to have the resources to carry out a *comprehensive* audit of the content of *all* disclosures they receive. A "comprehensive" audit would probably entail all of the following steps: checking for the internal consistency of information declared, comparing information declared across years, and cross-checking information declared with outside information. In the majority of cases, all of these steps are not feasible, because the volume of disclosures collected is extremely high, because only limited resources are available, or because agencies face both of those challenges. Moreover, verifying all disclosures received may not be an efficient allocation of resources.

How can this be reconciled with the fact that, for example, 27 percent of the jurisdictions in our survey that carry out verification select all disclosures for verification, as shown in figure 5.2? In some of these cases, verification is a single step, such as a check for internal consistency and plausibility. In other cases, the number of disclosures filed is small enough to allow for a comprehensive audit of all disclosures. In extremely rare cases, electronic tools allow the use of automatic verification processes and cross-checking with both public registries and information from financial institutions.

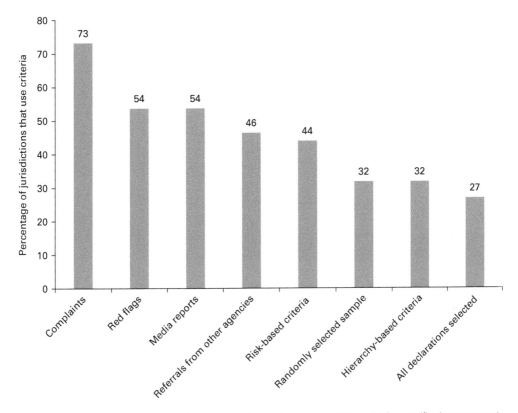

FIGURE 5.2 Selecting All Disclosures for Verification Is the Least Common Approach

Note: Approximate percentages based on the analysis of the 41 disclosure jurisdictions that have verification processes in this sample.

On the basis of the legislation and the practice of verification across multiple jurisdictions, the criteria used to select disclosures for verification include the following:

- Randomly selected sample (for example, a certain percentage of all disclosures filed regardless of who the filer is)
- High-risk sectors (for example, officials involved in such high-risk sectors as licensing, infrastructure, energy, and mining)
- High-risk functions (for example, officials carrying out financial management and procurement functions in different sectors)
- Hierarchy (for example, higher-level officials such as cabinet members, heads of institutions, and members of parliament)
- Red flags detected in earlier screening of information in disclosures (for example, inconsistencies found in the form, substantial variations in assets or income)
- Referral from another agency (for example, because of irregularities identified by the tax administration)

- Complaint or allegation (for example, information received by the agency from the public about either a position in a company or real estate that is not reflected on the form)
- Media reports (for example, a newspaper article that shows a photograph of a mansion that an official uses on a regular basis but that has not appeared in the financial disclosure).

Figure 5.2 shows that, among the criteria used for selecting disclosures for verification, complaints, red flags, media reports, and referrals from another agency are the most common. Focusing on high-risk positions and using a randomly selected sample are less so.

In those countries that have provisions on verification, routine checks are usually more prevalent than are irregular checks (see figure 5.3). This means that a *systematic approach* to verification (such as checking for inconsistencies and irregularities across a large number of disclosures, and focusing on a random sample of disclosures for in-depth review) is more widespread in financial disclosure legislation than is an an *ad hoc* approach (checking only when a complaint or notification from another agency

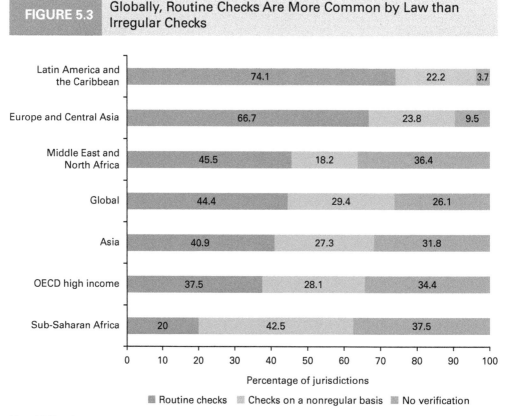

FIGURE 5.3 Globally, Routine Checks Are More Common by Law than Irregular Checks

Note: OECD = Organisation for Economic Co-operation and Development. Approximate percentages based on the analysis of 153 jurisdictions.

about a specific filer is received). However, this preference does not play out in practice, because among the surveyed countries, most actually carry out ad hoc verifications—in large part because of capacity constraints.

The survey data also show that, when selecting disclosures for verification, jurisdictions rely on more than one of the criteria. For example, jurisdictions use a combination of the following:

- Risk-based, hierarchy-based, red flags, and media reports
- Randomly selected sample, hierarchy-based, red flags, complaints, media reports, and risk-based
- Red flags, referrals from another agency, complaints, and media reports
- Risk-based, hierarchy-based, red flags, referrals, complaints, and media reports.

Let's see what one of these mixes of criteria could looks like when implemented. In this case, we will consider the combination of randomly selected sample, hierarchy-based, red flags, complaints, media reports, and risk-based criteria.

Random Sample

For example, about 4 percent of all disclosures, which would be randomly selected, could be subject to a full review (for example, for internal consistency, or cross-checks with registries and government databases, such as that of the tax administration). The disclosures reviewed would be selected even if no complaints were received and no preliminary irregularities were identified in terms of variations of wealth. The seniority of the filer would be irrelevant. Using a random sample approach can be particularly useful in financial disclosure systems that have a large number of filers and that include different levels of filers: high level and mid level; or high, mid, and low levels. In this way, the verification system can create a deterrent effect throughout the entire pool of filers.

Hierarchy-Based Criteria

Regardless of which officials are identified through the other criteria, disclosures of high-level officials are selected for verification. For example, the disclosures of cabinet members, deputy ministers, and heads of institutions such as the tax administration are always subject to in-depth review.

Red Flags

The red flags considered relevant for deciding which disclosures to verify can vary:

- Red flags in the submitted form (for example, large values of liabilities owed to individuals or close family members; high values of income from consultancies, or from sources such as gifts and inheritances)
- Red flags resulting from comparing the content of disclosures over time (for example, inconsistencies between the variation in assets and income across years,

after accounting for liabilities; substantial variations in assets, liabilities, and income across years)

- Red flags resulting from checks with outside sources of information. (For example, a disclosure agency could compare the list of filers with names listed in the company registry to help identify discrepancies between high-level positions in the private sector that were either declared or omitted and the data in the company registry.)

Allegations (Complaints or Notifications) from the Public and Media Reports

Some agencies use allegations received from the public or through media reports as immediate triggers for in-depth verification. Although in some systems, all allegations from the public trigger in-depth verification, this is not the case everywhere. In some cases, agencies receive a massive number of allegations and thus must screen and prioritize them for review. The availability and extent of public access to disclosures can also play an important role in the reliability and usefulness to the verification process of the information that is received from the public and from media reports.

Risk-Based Criteria

This approach is based on the assumption that certain positions, institutions, and roles or functions expose a filer to a greater risk of corruption or conflicts of interest. For example, the disclosures of the following categories of filers could be selected for enhanced scrutiny:

- Filers with decision-making authority in high-value public tenders
- Filers with responsibilities for major transactions with state property and resources (such as contracts for the extraction and use of natural resources, or for privatization)
- Filers working in institutions or departments with irregularities (for example, based on reports of the Supreme Audit Authority)
- Filers with licensing and regulatory responsibilities in strategic sectors (such as banking, energy, and telecommunications)
- Filers who occupy positions that have been connected to corruption (that is, officials who previously occupied that position were prosecuted for corruption offenses)
- Positions considered high risk on the basis of money-laundering typologies (such as those that have corruption as a predicate offense)
- Positions considered high risk on the basis of the domestic risk analysis in other sectors (such as taxation)
- Filers in positions whose previous occupants received sanctions for financial disclosure violations.

This mix of criteria (that is, a combination of a randomly selected sample, hierarchy-based criteria, red flags, complaints, media reports, and risk-based criteria) would not necessarily be applicable in most verification systems. The following considerations might help practitioners choose the right mix for their jurisdictions—and ultimately, how many disclosures could receive an in-depth review:

- The number of filers
- The time and resources required for in-depth verification of one disclosure
- The availability of staff members for verification and their skill level. (Even if a high number of staff members can be dedicated to verification, they may still need to acquire relevant skills, such as financial analysis, or an understanding of the different implications for conflicts of interest or the purposes of different types of investment tools.)
- Whether filing systems are paper based or electronic
- The degree of automation of verification processes. (Filing disclosures electronically and transferring information to a database do not necessarily automate the verification process. Identifying irregularities and red flags in a single disclosure cycle or across time requires putting in place operations and formulas, and/or ensuring access to information in public registries and government databases.)
- Ease of identification of high-risk filers, such as those with decision-making authority in high-value public tenders.

The Verification Process

Verification can include a broad menu of methods:

- Checking for internal consistency and plausibility within the information disclosed in one form
- Comparing the official's disclosures across different years
- Checking that the items declared (such as positions and stock ownership) are compatible with the official's mandate and do not raise conflict of interest issues
- Cross-checking with information held by other public entities (for example, the real estate register, the tax authority database, the customs database, and so on)
- Cross-checking with information held by private entities (for example, bank transactions or contracts)
- Requesting clarifications or documents from the official (such as invoices, contracts, and salary slips) that are necessary to complete verification
- Conducting "lifestyle checks" of consistency between information declared and the standard of living of the officials (through onsite visits to their home or other examinations).

Not all of these processes need to occur in parallel. The first step could involve screening a large number of disclosures for inconsistencies (such as variations in income across years or substantial differences between variations in income and assets acquired across years). Once the pool of disclosures has been

> Not all methods identified in the verification process need to occur at the same time.

narrowed down, the second step could be to focus on the disclosures that present inconsistencies and to cross-check the information declared with information held by other entities (such as company registries or tax administration data).

The data in figure 5.4 illustrate that countries use a variety of verification methods. Among them, cross-checking with public sources, comparing content across years, and requesting clarification from the official are the most widespread. Often, more than one verification method is used. For example, one agency compares the content of the form across different years, checks items declared for potential conflicts of interest, cross-checks information declared with information held by public and private entities, and requests clarifications from the official. In another country, the mix of verification methods includes comparing disclosures across years, checking items declared for potential conflicts of interest, and requesting clarifications from the official.

Numerous factors determine how many methods an agency uses during the verification process and how many disclosures are actually included in the process. In some of the jurisdictions in which we have worked, the option of cross-checking disclosed information with information held by private entities (such as bank transactions) is not included in the authorizing legislation. Indeed, in one jurisdiction, after the implementation of the financial disclosure legislation, we saw a bank secrecy law enacted that limited the access of the disclosure agency to bank records of any kind without a court order. In other cases, cross-checking of disclosed information with data from registries

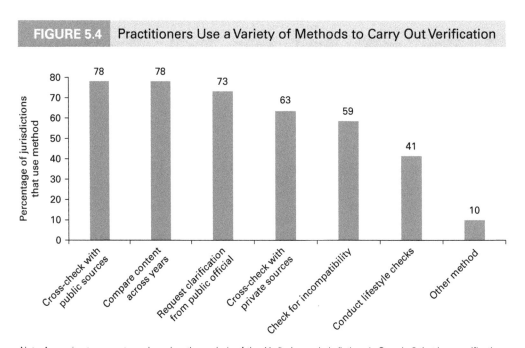

FIGURE 5.4 Practitioners Use a Variety of Methods to Carry Out Verification

Note: Approximate percentages based on the analysis of the 41 disclosure jurisdictions in Sample 2 that have verification processes.

or public entities can be accomplished for only a limited number of disclosures because the data are not available in an electronic format or are not centralized; thus requests must be sent to each regional branch of the registry.

If disclosures are filed on paper, checks for internal consistency or comparisons across years for a large number of disclosures are feasible for only a smaller number of disclosures than is possible if disclosures are filed electronically. Another factor that plays an important role is whether any of the activities carried out during verification are automated. According to data from our survey of 52 jurisdictions, about 29 percent of the 41 jurisdictions that have a verification system in place automate some of the processes they use as part of verification. It is unlikely that automated procedures are used outside of this sample of jurisdictions.

If a disclosure system is not carrying out all the operations mentioned or if it is not able to process a lot of disclosures through these operations, it does not necessarily mean that the system is not effective. As noted earlier, gradual implementation is key: indeed, a marathon—not a sprint—is the most appropriate metaphor for implementation. In other words, a complex verification system is not created overnight, and many of the required variables are either not dependent or dependent to a very small degree on the disclosure agency (for example, how information is made available by public registries, or the quality of that information). Moreover, particularly in the early stages of a financial disclosure system, a gradual approach is important because other building blocks of the system need to be in place before verification can be effective: a strong collection system, an effective process to ensure compliance with the obligation to disclose, and a blank form that asks the questions relevant for the verification process. In many cases, establishing all of these foundational elements early on in the financial disclosure system leaves little time for verification.

What Happens When Irregularities Are Found?

The verification process is shaped by the mandate and objectives of the financial disclosure agency. When irregularities are found, several responses are possible:

> The verification process is shaped by the mandate and objectives of the financial disclosure agency.

- Imposing administrative sanctions based on the findings of the verification process
- Forwarding the results of the work to other institutions for sanctioning and follow-up
- Sending notifications to law enforcement bodies for further investigation or prosecution.[3]

There is a different level of depth and complexity involved in the process for an agency that is responsible for imposing sanctions either directly or indirectly than there is for an agency that is responsible for producing analysis and for identifying red flags to be followed up in detail by other institutions. Indeed, how far along in the process of verification/imposing sanctions an agency is required to go will determine the desired capacity. For instance, an agency that is responsible for building a case or applying sanctions will require more capacity than will an agency responsible solely for basic screening.

Public Access and Verification

Three possible scenarios illustrate the relationship between public access and verification in a disclosure system. In certain systems, public access to the content of disclosures functions alongside verification processes, complementing them. In other systems, verification processes take place in the absence of mechanisms for public access. The third scenario involves a system that has public access but no verification. Figure 5.5 shows the percentage of existing systems with these scenarios.

In terms of improving the verification system,[4] the first scenario, in which public access and verification complement each other, is preferable. When some or all of the content of financial disclosures is made publicly available, it is as if the disclosure agency increases its human resources free of charge. For example, in countries that have both public access and verification in place, as soon as the content of disclosures becomes publicly available, the media and nongovernmental organizations start scrutinizing the content. Although it can be difficult for the staff of the disclosure agency in the capital to determine whether the head of customs in a rural region lives beyond his means, it can be a rather simple task for a journalist living and working in the region. At the community level, the fact that the head of customs lives in a big mansion, which started being built soon after the official was promoted, is in many cases not a very well-kept secret.

In such a scenario, the value added is most significant when civil society, investigative journalists, and the public can have easy access to the information in disclosures through,

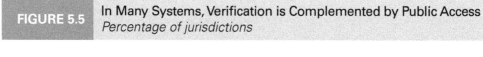

FIGURE 5.5   In Many Systems, Verification is Complemented by Public Access
Percentage of jurisdictions

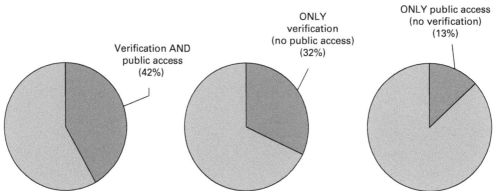

Verification AND
public access
(42%)

ONLY
verification
(no public access)
(32%)

ONLY public access
(no verification)
(13%)

Note: Approximate percentages based on the analysis of 153 jurisdictions.

for example, an online system. In jurisdictions that provide access to much of the data included in the disclosures and that make those data easily accessible, practitioners report the most significant benefits for the verification process. However, as figure 5.6 illustrates, there is still room for growth in implementing verification and online public access.

However, this does not mean that verification cannot be effective without public access to information. The main difference is that a very powerful verification tool is not at the disposal of the practitioners. Moreover, as discussed in depth in chapter 6 (on public access), the benefit to the verification process is not the only variable to consider when establishing public access. Indeed, public access can benefit the financial disclosure system in many other ways.

Finally, some countries have adopted the third scenario, in which public access (sometimes very extensive) is in place, but without any institutionalized verification mechanism. The expectation in this scenario is that civil society and the media will perform some monitoring of the content of disclosures. Moreover, institutions such as the prosecutor's office and other investigative bodies may use financial disclosures in their broader anticorruption activities. Although civil society and the media may identify irregularities and inconsistencies in a number of cases, they do not have the same effectiveness as a public institution carrying out a verification mandate, because, among other limitations, they do not have access to nonpublic registries and databases. At the same time, although the prosecutor's office and other investigative bodies may use financial disclosures in their broader anticorruption work, they do not have a mandate to scrutinize the content of the disclosures in the absence of suspicion of corruption offenses.

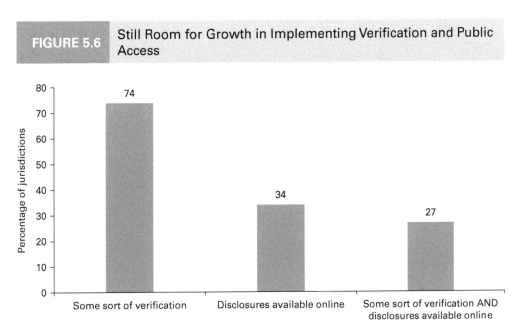

FIGURE 5.6 Still Room for Growth in Implementing Verification and Public Access

Note: Approximate percentages based on the analysis of 153 jurisdictions.

Interagency Cooperation for Effective Verification

Mapping Sources of Information for Verification (Domestically and Abroad)

Access to reliable registries, databases, and—more broadly—information from public and private sector entities is a useful tool in determining the ability of the verification system to deliver substantial results.

Information from such sources can be useful for different verification processes. For example, company registries can be useful for checking whether activities or stock ownership declared by public officials is compatible with their mandate. The database of the tax administration, as well as the property and vehicle registries can be useful for cross-checking that the information declared in the forms is consistent with the information held by those entities (for example, there is nothing that was omitted, over-declared, or declared with some inaccuracies). Information from financial institutions can help identify whether all bank accounts or other forms of investment have been truthfully disclosed.

Information from supreme audit institutions or agencies that monitor public tenders can be useful in a comprehensive audit of a financial disclosure, as well as in identifying which financial disclosures should be considered high risk and given priority in the verification process. For example, a financial disclosure agency may use reports from supreme audit institutions to identify specific public sector institutions where irregularities have been found and apply greater scrutiny to the disclosures of officials from such institutions. At the same time, the information in a particular audit can contribute to the verification of the content of disclosures.

A useful exercise in support of the verification process is mapping all of the sources of information that can be relevant to the categories required in the disclosure. For example, consider answers to the question, what source of information can you rely on to cross-check the information declared in section X (for example, real estate)? See figure 5.7.

In many jurisdictions, officials need to declare assets that are held domestically as well as in foreign jurisdictions. Consequently, other questions that might emerge during the mapping exercise is, what are the relevant sources of information abroad, and what is the process for obtaining such information?

Open source information (available to the public online either for free or through payment of an access fee) is invaluable to financial disclosure practitioners. In some jurisdictions, real property records and company registries can be accessed online (for example, in Hong Kong SAR, China). In addition to subnational and national company registries, there are some privately owned supranational resources that aggregate information from multiple jurisdictions, which may further facilitate access to relevant information.

FIGURE 5.7   Sources of Information for Verification

Property registry	Vehicle registry	Company registry
Customs	Supreme audit institutions	Agencies that monitor public tenders
Financial intelligence unit	Financial institutions	Tax administration

However, using such sources of information raises some practical challenges that need to be taken into consideration. For example, in some countries with federal systems, company registries or real property records are not centralized at the national level. The same problem arises in the case of real estate records, which may be available only at the local level (for example, at the city level).

Financial disclosure agencies do not have at their disposal the same international cooperation avenues as financial intelligence units (FIUs), police, or prosecutors do. This limits the options available for receiving information or intelligence about assets held abroad. However, this constraint does not preclude a disclosure agency from contacting foreign counterparts for guidance on open source information or other databases that may be available.

Prioritizing Sources of Information

Once the sources of information for verification have been mapped, the next step is to prioritize them. For example, a company registry might be useful for cross-checking information on public officials in high-level positions in the private sector. However, there may be some serious practical challenges to consider. For example, the information in the registry might be available only in paper copies obtained through personal visits to the offices of the company registry. Or, as is the case in some countries, the information from one registry may be readily available to the agency, whereas access to other information may require a written request or court order. These variables should be taken into consideration when mapping and prioritizing sources. As illustrated in figure 5.8, there are some common variables.

FIGURE 5.8 | Prioritization Variables

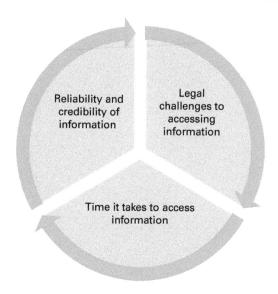

AreThere Any Legal Challenges to Accessing the Information?

In many countries, information from financial institutions and from the tax administration cannot be obtained during the verification process for financial disclosures. In a very limited number of countries, information from financial institutions—in particular, bank account information—can be obtained, but only if there is an indication that some irregularity has taken place (for example, an allegation indicating inaccuracies in the disclosure, or unjustified variations in wealth). Tax administration information may sometimes be available for cross-checking purposes even before any irregularities or red flags have been identified.

Information received by FIUs from financial institutions (such as suspicious transaction reports), as well as the analytical work carried out by FIUs, is frequently cited by disclosure practitioners as a potentially useful source of information in the verification process. The main impediment to disclosure agencies accessing this information stems from limitations in FIU mandates to disseminate analytical work only to law enforcement bodies to be used in anti-money-laundering cases.

How Long Does ItTake to Access Information?

The time required to access information depends on two factors—the format of the information and the mechanism for access.

Whether the information can be accessed in paper or electronic format plays an important role in the prioritization exercise. Unless the number of filers is quite small, paper records from registries or other sources are not accessed for routine checks of all disclosures. Despite the time required, they could be used when a comprehensive analysis of disclosure content is carried out for the highest-risk disclosures, or when there is a preliminary indication of inaccuracies.

The process of accessing information can provide an indication of its length. Some of the scenarios we have encountered include the following:

- Disclosure agency staff members have direct access to the electronic database of a registry or another public institution.
- Disclosure agency staff members must make a formal request in writing to a central entity to receive specific information.
- Disclosure agency staff members must make a formal request in writing to all the regional branches of an institution. (This situation happens in cases where information is not centralized nationally. To obtain relevant information, the agency must reach out to all of the regional and local branches of the property registry or the tax administration.)

The rule of thumb in terms of prioritization in these scenarios is similar to the one in the discussion of paper versus electronic format; the longer it takes to access information, the less often that information should be used for large numbers of disclosures.

How Reliable and Credible Is the Information?

Practitioners should consider whether the value of the information is worth the expenditure of resources necessary to obtain the information. For example, in some systems, real property or company registries may be unreliable as a consequence of missing records, notoriously inaccurate information, or improper storage of records.

Ensuring Effective Interagency Cooperation

Investing in interagency cooperation brings substantial dividends to the verification process. As the preceding discussion indicates, the verification process may depend on institutions outside the financial disclosure agency (see box 5.1). Memoranda of understanding among agencies may be useful for clarifying the process to be used for requesting and accessing information. Regular discussions among practitioners from the financial disclosure agency and other entities may also support effective cooperation.

Such regular interactions can build trust, as well as an understanding of the detailed operational needs and limitations of each institution. They represent good opportunities to understand how processes for accessing information can be streamlined and can evolve where there are unexplored synergies. For example, financial disclosure practitioners can find out about and can quickly benefit from any transitions to electronic databases or from any changes in the way information is organized that are being implemented in other institutions. These regular interactions can also be useful for understanding the bottlenecks in cooperation that can be dealt with exclusively by amending legislation.

BOX 5.1　Verifying Abroad: International Cooperation and Open Sources

The percentage of agencies currently sharing information with other disclosure agencies abroad, even on an ad hoc basis, is very low. However, as countries build effective verification systems, they repeatedly stumble over the difficulties in verifying assets and interests that public officials hold abroad. Formal (mutual legal assistance) or informal (intelligence) information-exchange channels generally exist to facilitate the gathering of information for criminal cases;[a] thus, they may not seem to be the most obvious avenue by which to gather information for verification of disclosures, which is an administrative procedure. Though in some countries, the verification process can lead to criminal charges, verification is still largely an administrative process. Once the verification process shows evidence of potential criminal offenses, the majority of financial disclosure agencies forward the case to prosecutors to carry on with the formal investigation.

Very few countries have resorted to the use of open source information, which involves finding, selecting, and acquiring information from publicly available resources. However, it does not eliminate the need to contact colleagues abroad. For example, the requesting financial disclosure agency may not know that a certain open source exists, or may be unsure about the quality of the information, or may need support to understand how the information is structured. In these cases, contacting the financial disclosure agency of the target country may provide important guidance on how to make the best use of open source information.

In other cases, the financial disclosure agency may need information to which the financial disclosure agency in another country has routine access. In a simple example, Country A, as part of its verification process, has access to the property registry. Country B needs to check whether a public official has property in Country A. If information-exchange channels exist, the agency in Country B can reach out to its counterpart in Country A and check the information easily.

Certainly there are more complicated scenarios, in which an agency might not have direct access to the information requested. However, neither this situation nor others similar to it preclude the possibility of establishing information-exchange channels.

As a recent study on the feasibility of an international instrument for data exchange points out, there are three ways in which data exchange can be structured: by a multilateral convention, by an executive or administrative agreement, or by a bilateral or multilateral memorandum of understanding (Hoppe 2014). All of these options involve different levels of complexity and political support. In all cases, the instrument would need to detail the objective and scope of the agreement, the information covered, the restrictions on use of information, and the possibility of declining the request, as well as the confidentiality, data protection, costs, language, and so on.[b]

a. For more on existing international cooperation, please see Brun and others (2011), chapter 7.
b. For the draft memorandum of understanding proposed by the study, please see http://www.respaweb.eu/11/library#respa-publications-and-research-18.

(continued next page)

Using Electronic Tools in the Verification Process

Countries are increasingly considering greater automation or the incorporation of electronic tools at various points in the financial disclosure process. As mentioned earlier, transitioning to an electronic process can aid in disclosure by (a) creating an online database of filers to ease the burden of filing and storing disclosures; (b) providing online submission for filers to simplify the process for the officials as well as the collecting agency; or (c) creating an automated verification system to help identify red flags or even single out suspicious disclosures. Also worth noting is that, although monitoring and evaluation of the overall financial disclosure system is far off for most countries, the implementation of electronic data management can ultimately facilitate better internal analytics and intelligence. Such information can serve to further improve upon existing systems. Although such tools can be very useful, the challenges presented by greater automation should be understood.

An electronic component can be incorporated into the financial disclosure process at varying levels of comprehensiveness and complexity. When considering a move to automation, it is important that the agency considers its capacity to work with the data and the quality of the data received from filers. For example, automated verification systems based on risk factors and red flags may be implemented. The system can be set up to identify disclosures for further inspection on the basis of, for example, the fact that the purchase price of a vehicle appears excessive relative to an official's income. An automated search such as this could result in more thorough examination and could make it possible to conduct a greater number of verifications each year, but it would require designing the disclosure form in a way that makes this information easily searchable. If the end goal is to automate the verification process, it is imperative that the transition process (or the original design, in new systems) focus first on the financial disclosure system's foundation—the form.

Even if a jurisdiction has a fully electronic submission process, its impact may be limited if there is no systematic process by which the disclosures filed electronically can be verified. In such cases, although the submission process might be more efficient, once the disclosures reach the disclosure agency for verification or compliance checks, they hit a bottleneck. Only a small number of disclosures are selected, then printed as hard copies, and finally sent to the verification team for further analysis. Although it is helpful to transition to electronic tools at any stage of the process, it is nonetheless imperative to consider all aspects of the disclosure system.

A common challenge to full automation of the verification process is the ability to compare the information in disclosures with information in external databases to identify irregularities. The ability to do so electronically could significantly increase the number of false disclosures identified during the verification process because the cross-checking of information would be performed on all disclosures received, rather than on the number presently cross-checked manually. However, this requires the information to be standardized across all databases and that the agency gain access to the necessary external databases; both of these requirements are rarely met.

Finally, there are two real and difficult legal hurdles in transitioning to a fully electronic and automated system. First, as mentioned earlier, the disclosure agency should have access to external databases such as those from the registries, the tax office, and banks. Often, financial disclosure agencies are not granted access; if they are granted access, they are required to solicit the information on a case-by-case basis. In both scenarios, automated verification is not possible. Bank account information is even more challenging. With bank secrecy laws in place in many countries, the information held by banks is not accessible without a court order or an active investigation. Second, regarding the submission process, in order to submit a disclosure electronically and have it recognized as a legal document, one must be able to use a digital signature. Although this is a capacity issue, it is also a legal one that often requires legislation to establish the legal status of a digital signature. Without a digital signature, forms can be submitted online, but a hard copy is still required and any further verification must be conducted on the hard copy, thus negating many of the benefits created by filing online.

Financial disclosure is increasingly using electronic and automated systems. Although this transition is undoubtedly a positive development for financial disclosure as a whole, it is vital that the foundations of the system are not overlooked. In order to automate a system effectively, all aspects of the process must function well and should be designed in a way that facilitates the transition to fully electronic and automated systems.

Chapter 5—Key Recommendations

- Verification should be a primary focus when implementing an effective financial disclosure system. It is a pivotal process during which real value can be extracted from the information or data collected.

- The primary objective of the verification process should be to ensure that filers have submitted accurate information—that the data declared reflect reality and are complete.

(continued next page)

- Expectations of the verification process should be pragmatic. Numerous elements, such as a strong disclosure form and reliable registries and databases for cross-checking information, are necessary to enable verification to deliver substantial results. Managing expectations is important, because many of the elements are outside the financial disclosure agency's control.

- Regardless of the level of resources available, building an effective verification system can and should be a priority. Adopting a risk-based approach or prioritizing sources of information can help deliver results with limited resources.

- The selection of disclosures for verification should be guided by criteria that both work within the constraints of the available resources and further the objectives of the system. Such options may include randomly selected samples, hierarchy of filers, red flags, complaints, media reports, risk-based criteria, and referrals from other agencies.

- Country experience indicates that there should be some level of public access to the content of the disclosures. However, verification processes can be strong even in the absence of such access.

- Interagency cooperation should be encouraged and should be an integral part of a successful financial disclosure system.

- Incorporating electronic tools can enhance and broaden the scope and effectiveness of the verification process.

Notes

1. For more information on the misuse of corporate vehicles, see van der Does de Willebois and others (2011).
2. For more information on including beneficial ownership information in the blank form, see chapter 3 of this Guide.
3. For more in-depth analysis on sanctioning, see chapter 7 of this Guide.
4. The debate about public access goes beyond the benefits to the verification process; see chapter 6 of this Guide.

References

Brun, J.-P., L. Gray, C. Scott, and K. M. Stephenson. 2011. *Asset Recovery Handbook: A Guide for Practitioners.* Washington, DC: World Bank.

Hoppe, Tilman. "Feasibility Study on an International Instrument on Data Exchange for Income and Asset Declarations." 2014. ReSPA (Regional School of Public Administration), Danilovgrad, Montenegro.

van der Does de Willebois, E., E. M. Halter, R. A. Harrison, J. W. Park, and J. C. Sharman. 2011. *The Puppet Masters: How the Corrupt Use Legal Structures to Hide Stolen Assets and What to Do about It.* Washington, DC: World Bank.

6. Why and How to Provide Access to Information in Disclosures

A journalist once became curious about the luxurious cars that a high-level public official was driving to work. When trying to access his disclosure to see if there was any information on the vehicles, the journalist learned that disclosures were shared only with the consent of the official. Furthermore, he needed to submit a form explaining his reason for wanting to access the information. Needless to say, the public official never gave consent and the disclosure remained confidential. The journalist met a dead end. In other countries, looking at the form of the public official would require only an Internet connection.

Without a doubt, the availability of information from public officials' disclosures is one of the most sensitive decisions in the development of a disclosure system. Disclosure systems generally aim to promote transparency and accountability; however, the degree of transparency of declared data ignites heated debate.

Although it might seem that sharing declared information with the public is the epitome of promoting transparency, it is not that straightforward in practice. The declared information refers to assets and interests that public officials have in their private capacity, raising questions about privacy and security. Therefore, it is almost inevitable that debates will arise on theoretical questions such as the following: How private is the life of a public official? Should officials be held to the same standards of privacy as are regular citizens when they have a public responsibility? Are security concerns strong enough to override information-sharing?

This chapter will not resolve these debates.[1] A country's culture, context, and regulatory framework heavily influence how the issue of transparency is approached. Instead, this chapter focuses on practical considerations in implementing public access to disclosures, while providing fresh data on the state and nuances of information-sharing worldwide.

This chapter addresses a connected set of questions: Should all the information in disclosures be made public? How is an agency to select what information should remain confidential? How accessible will the information be? What will the procedures be for accessing the information? How is an agency to approach sharing information with other public agencies? The chapter will also address other more practical aspects that are key to, yet generally overlooked, in the debate about public access.

It is important to note that addressing the issue of public access requires a fundamental conceptual clarification. Sharing information from disclosures has two distinct sides: one, which is the more obvious, is sharing information with the general public; the other is sharing information with other institutions and agencies. Sharing information with these different audiences involves different objectives and demands different approaches, as detailed further in this chapter.

Public Availability of Information

Some common arguments that favor sharing information with the public (see figure 6.1) are the following:

- Academic studies have shown that public access to declared information is associated with lower levels of perceived corruption (Djankov and others 2009).

> Openness can be a good antidote to cheating by lowering the proclivity to lie.

- Public availability can reinforce scrutiny. Making information available to all adds an endless number of eyes that can double-check the disclosures of public officials. This way, outside parties—notably, the media and civil society organizations—can help government agencies in their task of ensuring the integrity and validity of the data.
- Public availability can increase the deterrent effect of disclosure systems. There is no better deterrent to wrongdoing than the increased likelihood of being caught.

FIGURE 6.1 Weighing the Arguments of Public Availability

Public access not only facilitates detection of irregularities but also can add a layer of public shame for the wrongdoer.

- Access to information can also raise the stakes for the disclosure agency, as its results can become a matter of public scrutiny. Information on the agency's work—such as the number of disclosures verified, compliance rates, and sanctions imposed—is mutually reinforcing and can promote greater effectiveness.

Some of the arguments against public disclosure include the following:

- In some countries, public access to disclosures can be seen as an invasion of an official's privacy, which some argue can become a barrier to participating in the public sector.
- In countries with security concerns, officials believe that disclosure of personal addresses may threaten their (and their family's) personal safety or that the information may be used to inform ransom demands in areas where kidnappings are common.

As both sides raise valid arguments, it may be useful instead to focus on the underlying objective of publicly sharing the information disclosed. That objective helps inform the appropriate approach for a financial disclosure system.

Approaches to Public Availability

Broadly speaking, information-sharing options tend to narrow down to one of the following approaches: choosing public availability (either by making all the information from disclosures accessible to the general public or by publishing only some of the data), or taking the path of confidentiality (by opting not to make anything public). Among surveyed countries, slightly more than half (55 percent) require the declared information to be public, with either full or partial access to it. Regionally, it is possible to see that public availability is quite widespread in OECD high-income countries and in Europe and Central Asia (see figure 6.2).

Further analysis shows that public availability of the information by law is directly correlated with income. As figure 6.3 shows, the higher the income of the country, the higher the chances that it makes the disclosures public by law.

Taking a position on the publicity versus confidentiality debates is not the end of the important decision making on this topic. Unless the path of full and unrestricted publicity is chosen, other implementation decisions must be made. Two fundamental questions help clarify some of the details yet to be tackled:

- What information will be made available? That is, how much or how little information will be public? And which criteria will determine what is finally made public?
- How accessible will the data be? That is, where will the public find the data? And what will be the procedures for accessing them?

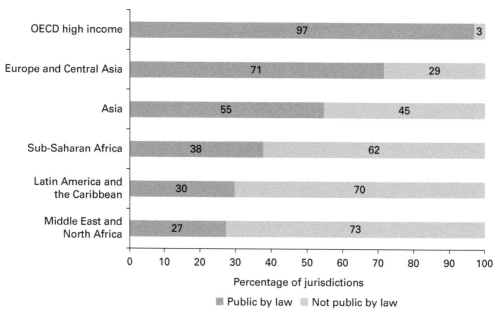

FIGURE 6.2 Declared Information Is Publicly Available by Law, by Region

Percentage of jurisdictions

■ Public by law ■ Not public by law

Note: OECD = Organisation for Economic Co-operation and Development. Approximate percentages based on the analysis of 153 jurisdictions.

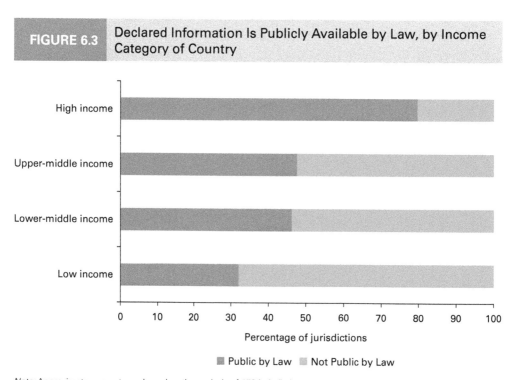

FIGURE 6.3 Declared Information Is Publicly Available by Law, by Income Category of Country

Percentage of jurisdictions

■ Public by Law ■ Not Public by Law

Note: Approximate percentages based on the analysis of 153 jurisdictions.

What Information Is Made Available?

Disclosure agencies make a range of information available to the public and to other agencies.

Information Contained in Public Officials' Declarations

The range of information made available is broad, ranging from those systems that share all available information without any filter to those that share only a two-line summary. Current practices show a tendency to make some of the information public, with 42 percent of jurisdictions sharing only parts of the disclosure, and 15 percent sharing all the information declared.[2] This trend indicates that countries often try to prioritize transparency while attempting to appease objections linked to privacy and security. Two approaches are commonly used to determine which information is made publicly available.

Approach 1: Basing the Decision on the Content of the Declaration Form

In this approach, the main criterion is the type of information. In the context of a country, some information is considered private or too sensitive and should remain hidden from the public eye. For example, this might mean sharing the names of banks where an official holds accounts and liabilities, but not the account numbers. Another example is publishing the value and location of real estate assets, but not the address of the official's personal residence.

Finding the right mix of information to share and to protect is challenging. In all instances, it is important to avoid using the need to protect certain information as an excuse to curtail information-sharing. Transparency should be the priority, and even when some information remains protected, the idea is to grant access to as much information as possible to ensure transparency and the ability of the public to scrutinize the disclosure forms.

Approach 2: Basing the Decision on the Type of Public Official

In contrast to the first approach, the main criterion here is the type of filer. The decision to publish the information is based entirely on the hierarchy or type of function that the public official performs. For example, in certain countries, only disclosures from high-level public officials are public.[3] The type of official may also determine the mode in which the information is made accessible. For example, the agency may choose to publish the disclosures from high-level public officials online while making the disclosures of lower-level officials accessible only at the agency.

These two approaches can be complementary. Some countries choose a combination of the two to ensure public access while taking into account valid concerns. See figure 6.4 for some of these approaches to public access.

FIGURE 6.4 Approaches for Public Access

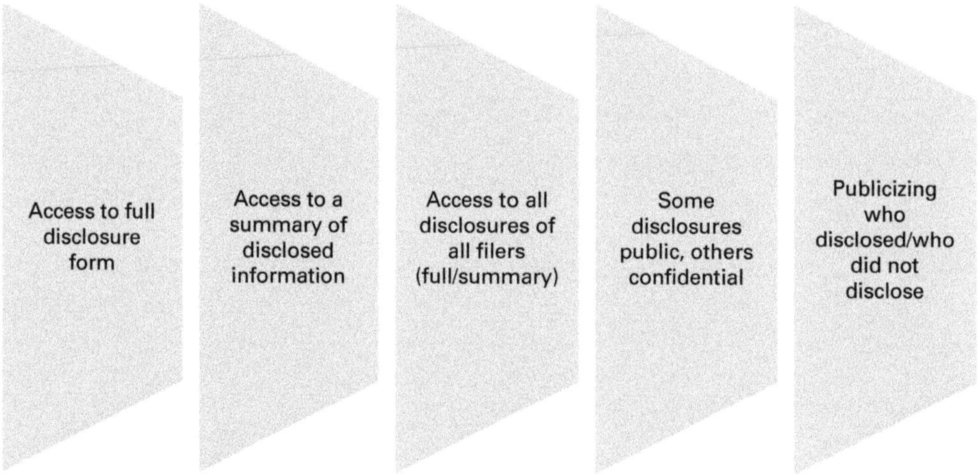

Access to full disclosure form	Access to a summary of disclosed information	Access to all disclosures of all filers (full/summary)	Some disclosures public, others confidential	Publicizing who disclosed/who did not disclose

Sharing Information about the Disclosure System

An often overlooked aspect of making disclosures public is the added value of providing information about the disclosure process itself, which shows that the disclosure agency is also subject to standards of information-sharing. In other words, the agency leads by example by being transparent about its work.

Sharing information about key elements of the disclosure process, such as dates and locations designated for submissions, as well as available support resources, can not only help in the process itself but also raise awareness and build credibility.

Furthermore, sharing information about the work of the disclosure agency—by publishing data on the compliance rates, the number of cases selected for analysis, the number of cases forwarded to prosecutors, and the administrative sanctions applied—can strengthen support for the system, build its credibility, and improve its efficiency. Most important, sharing these data can help reinforce the commitment to promoting transparency and integrity at all stages of the process.

How Accessible Will the Data Be?

The idea of making disclosures publicly available is not only about the actual information shared, but also about *how* it is shared—more specifically, how genuine the effort is to make the information available to and accessible by the public. The question here is, what defines a genuine effort? Here are examples of types of public access to information:

- Declarations are accessible upon request made in person, through postal mail, or by e-mail, after which a copy of the disclosure is sent by mail.

- Declarations are accessible only in person at the disclosure agency on Mondays and Wednesdays between 10:00 AM and 12:00 PM. The requesting individual must make a formal appointment and must provide his or her name, national identification number (for example, social security number), the purpose of requesting the information, and an explanation of what the information will be used for. Walk-ins are not accepted.
- Declarations are published in the official gazette, which is made available at the national library.
- Declarations are public, but for each request received, the public official in question must provide consent before the particulars of his or her disclosure are shared (and may decline the request, making the disclosure confidential).
- Disclosures are available online. However, it takes a skilled and determined person to figure out how to navigate the multiple pages required to locate the information.
- Declarations are public but can be seen only at the agency. No copies or photographs are permitted, and it is unlawful to disseminate the content of the disclosures in any way.
- Disclosures are available on the disclosure agency's website, which is searchable by name, position, agency, and other criteria. A secured copy of the disclosure can be downloaded to or printed from a personal computer.

These examples show a range of barriers to access. As a result, information that is technically public may be unavailable in practice.

The degree of accessibility can also determine whether all members of the public have equal access to the information. For example, if the forms can be accessed only in person at the disclosure agency, then only those people who can physically get to the agency have access. In a large country with such a requirement, a disclosure agency located only in the capital would severely limit the ability of those outside the city to access the information.

> The degree of accessibility can also determine whether all members of the public have equal access to the information.

How the information is made available also determines its usability. For instance, there is an obvious difference in usability between a photocopy of a handwritten form and a searchable website.

Recent trends show that countries are paying more attention to the issue of accessibility. In this sense, technology has opened up new possibilities. In a recent survey of disclosure implementation, countries mentioned the different ways in which they make information available, showing a growing trend in the use of electronic and online methods (see figure 6.5).

Recent trends are promising, but there is still room for growth for most countries in the area of accessibility. It is thus key to note that, upon deciding to share information with

FIGURE 6.5 Methods for Public Access to Disclosure Information

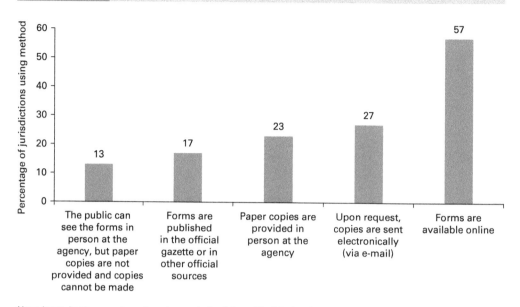

Note: Approximate percentages based on analysis of those 30 of the 52 disclosure jurisdictions in Sample 2 that provide access to the information in disclosures.

the public, practical implementation has major implications and will ultimately speak volumes as to the system's commitment to accessibility.

Common Implementation Challenges

Imagine that a disclosure agency receives 50,000 disclosures a year. The disclosures are submitted in paper format, and the agency scans each form and uploads it to a database. Each disclosure form has, on average, five pages and approximately 40 categories of information. Ten of those categories are not made public. Therefore, some personnel must be dedicated to scanning the forms as they arrive, and other personnel—with markers in hand—must be dedicated to manually striking out the nonpublic information before scanning the form so that it can be shared with the public. This agency has limited resources and therefore cannot perform any verification of the content of the disclosures, as most of its personnel are dedicated to processing the information.

Even well-meaning advocates of public availability may not have fully considered the resources needed for effective implementation. Human, technological, and financial resources are involved, not to mention ingenuity and creativity. While considering what and how information will be made public, it is also imperative to think about the logistics.

> While considering "what" and "how" information will be made public, it is also imperative to think about the logistics.

There are different methods for making information public that can be more or less labor intensive. For example, some countries decide to include the confidential information in a separate section, hence relying on the structure of the disclosure form to facilitate the data sorting. Others have already migrated to electronic filing, making it easier to automatically preserve the information. Still others, as mentioned before, rely on human resources to manually strike out the sensitive information.

Furthermore, one must consider the resources needed for access. If disclosures are made public only at the agency, then some personnel must be dedicated to interacting with customers. Alternatively, if the information is provided online, the number of information technology specialists might need to be increased.

These are just a few examples of the different aspects that should be considered when making information public in practice. In all cases, it is fundamental to assess the objective of making information public and then to adapt the implementation details to fit the available resources.

Sharing Information with Other Agencies and Institutions

The focus on the debate over public access to information often overshadows another fundamental aspect of information-sharing: ensuring that disclosure information contributes to the broader fight against corruption.

Practical experience shows that the issue of sharing information with other agencies is often overlooked, except in more established systems or when complaints call for it. However, it is actually this element that reveals the potential impact that disclosure systems can have.

Understanding the importance of sharing information comes with recognizing the value of the information provided in the disclosures. Some prefer to control the information and share only what is already public. Others believe that information exchange plays a role in the greater good of promoting integrity in the public sector. Anecdotal evidence suggests that the more the information in disclosures is used and shared, the more effective it is in preventing and detecting misconduct, and, ultimately, the more power it holds as an anticorruption mechanism.

Sharing Information with Other Government Agencies[4]

Financial disclosure is an important instrument on its own. However, it can also be a useful tool in the broader anticorruption fight by becoming a piece of a larger puzzle. For example, something as simple as a list of which public officials are required to file disclosures and—when available—the names of their dependents can help identify politically

> Financial disclosure can provide useful leads and may even become a piece of evidence in the investigation of corruption-related crimes.

exposed persons, as required under the Recommendations of the Financial Action Task Force (FATF).[5]

Other examples include a public official under investigation for bribery who testifies that the amount in question was a cash loan from an uncle. The relevant financial disclosure form would show whether the public official had declared either the cash or the loan (or had failed to do so), thereby aiding the investigation. Or, a disclosure form might provide useful information on the bank accounts and other financial instruments of a corrupt public official, thus helping to trace any stolen assets. But these are just a few examples. Whether through the information declared, the information omitted, or the variation in information across years, disclosures can provide useful leads and may even become evidence in the investigation of corruption-related crimes.

Information-sharing supports the wider use of the declared information by other agencies in their own work, thereby expanding the potential uses and value of disclosures. That said, it is important to keep in mind that sharing information from disclosures made to other government institutions should be seen as an independent process from providing public access. A disclosure agency can share information from completed disclosure forms with other public institutions, regardless of whether the forms are available to the general public.

This distinction is reflected in the data. Recent research shows that 42 percent[6] of the countries in the sample do not make disclosures available to the public; however, 94 percent[7] of the countries in the sample share at least part of the information with other government agencies.

Although a large percentage of the surveyed countries indicate that they share information, they do not share it in the same manner (figure 6.6). Among surveyed countries, 34 percent share disclosures with specific government agencies. Depending on the country, these agencies typically include financial intelligence units (FIUs), tax authorities, law enforcement agencies, other anticorruption institutions, control and auditing agencies, legal firms (prosecutors), courts, offices of the attorney general, or offices of the ombudsman.

However, upon closer review, it is worth noting that, although countries indicate that they share information with their counterparts, 38 percent require a condition to be met before they will provide the information. In most cases, the condition is a court order, judicial proceedings, or the existence of an ongoing investigation involving the public official.

In some cases, however, sharing information with FIUs, prosecutors, and other relevant parties may not require a court order, relying instead on a certain mechanism for coordination with that agency, usually in the form of an instrument such as a memorandum of understanding that establishes the basis for the information exchange.

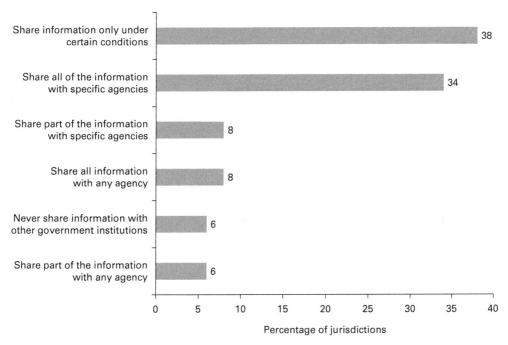

FIGURE 6.6 Conditions for Sharing Declared Information with Other Government Institutions

Share information only under certain conditions — 38

Share all of the information with specific agencies — 34

Share part of the information with specific agencies — 8

Share all information with any agency — 8

Never share information with other government institutions — 6

Share part of the information with any agency — 6

Percentage of jurisdictions

Note: Approximate percentages based on the analysis of 52 disclosure jurisdictions.

Sharing Information with Foreign and Private Sector Institutions

The term *politically exposed person* (PEP) is widely known among anti-money-laundering practitioners. It is generally used to denote individuals who are or have been entrusted with prominent public functions, such as heads of state or government, as well as their family members and close associates.[8] Depending on the country, there is often an important overlap between those officials who are required to submit a disclosure and those identified as PEPs.

Although most PEPs are free of corrupt practices, it is widely accepted that, as a result of their public functions, they are more vulnerable to abusing their positions and influence for personal gain. Indeed, PEPs may be more susceptible to carrying out corrupt acts, such as accepting and extorting bribes, misappropriating state assets, and using domestic and international financial systems to launder proceeds.[9] As a result, financial institutions[10] and other designated institutions[11] are encouraged, if not required, to treat them as high-risk customers.

PEPs—both foreign and domestic[12]—must undergo enhanced customer due diligence requirements when they open accounts and when they engage in financial transactions (for example, buying and selling real estate). These financial institutions are required to closely monitor their relationships with PEP customers and to report any suspicious activities to the relevant authorities.

Acknowledging that not all PEPs are, by definition, corrupt, but rather recognizing that they could be more susceptible to corrupt acts, this enhanced scrutiny of PEPs is a preventive approach. However, defining who exactly is a PEP in a given jurisdiction has been a contentious issue.

Despite efforts to clarify who is in a prominent public position, financial institutions generally struggle to determine which categories of public officials they must identify and monitor. In this sense, Rossi and others' (2012) publication, "Using Asset Disclosure for Identifying Politically Exposed Persons," which analyzes the ways in which financial disclosures can assist in identifying those officials who are considered to be in prominent public functions in a certain jurisdiction, may provide some much-needed guidance on this topic.

Furthermore, the information contained in the disclosure forms may also be used to conduct enhanced due diligence on PEPs by being a source of information for the ongoing monitoring of transactions of PEPs, verifying sources of wealth and funds, and assisting with the analysis of suspicious transaction reports.

In short, there are several opportunities in which both who declares and what is declared could be very useful for financial institutions in their aim to prevent and detect money laundering. However, disclosures can serve anti-money-laundering purposes only if the information is public or shared with financial institutions or with AML/CFT (anti-money-laundering and combating the financing of terrorism) authorities. Our experience shows that there is still a lot of room for improvement in this area. As figure 6.7 shows, 82 percent of the agencies in the sample stated that they do not share any information with financial institutions.

> Disclosures can only serve anti-money-laundering purposes if the information is public, or if the information is shared with financial institutions or with AML/CFT authorities.

Until a few years ago, the connection between financial disclosure and anti-money-laundering regimes went mostly undetected.[13] However, as both asset detection and AML/CFT regimes are strengthened, the connections are starting to appear more clearly in the view of practitioners. Furthermore, the connections and potential usefulness of disclosure for detecting and supporting the recovery of stolen assets are also starting to surface.

In the current global context, corrupt officials may hide assets abroad using complicated money-laundering schemes. Hidden assets are not very likely to appear in a financial disclosure. However, the failure to disclose these assets may be useful for arguing a case of illicit enrichment or even for private civil actions.[14] Furthermore, declared

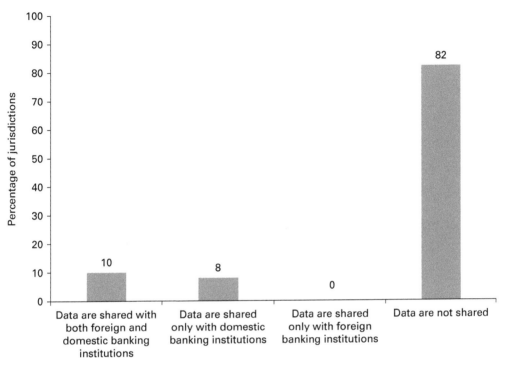

FIGURE 6.7

FIGURE 6.7 Methods for Sharing Disclosure Information with Banking Institutions in Relation to PEPs' Due Diligence Procedures

Percentage of jurisdictions

- Data are shared with both foreign and domestic banking institutions — 10
- Data are shared only with domestic banking institutions — 8
- Data are shared only with foreign banking institutions — 0
- Data are not shared — 82

Note: PEPs = politically exposed persons. Approximate percentages based on the analysis of 52 disclosure jurisdictions.

assets and bank accounts can be useful leads for establishing connections in a criminal investigation.

However, none of these potential uses of disclosures can be explored without some level of information exchange at the domestic and international levels. In this area, there is a lot of room for growth and exploration. As the data in figure 6.8 show, 35 percent of the agencies in the sample are unable to share information with foreign public institutions such as FIUs or prosecutors.

Most disclosure practitioners still tend to see the exchange of information with the general public and other institutions solely in light of how it can help achieve financial disclosure objectives. However, there is a positive growing trend to acknowledge the richness of the information in the disclosures and how it can serve other purposes. In sum, sharing information is certainly key to achieving the system's overall objectives, but it is also becoming a key piece of the broader anticorruption puzzle.

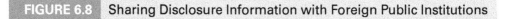

FIGURE 6.8 Sharing Disclosure Information with Foreign Public Institutions

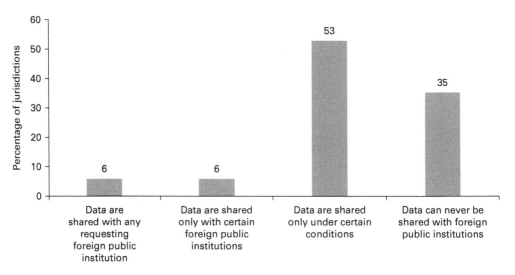

Note: Approximate percentages based on the analysis of 52 disclosure jurisdictions.

Chapter 6—Key Recommendations

- Sharing information from disclosures, in particular with the general public, is very important. It is also a delicate matter. Thus, culture, context, and the regulatory framework should be considered when determining how transparency is approached.

- When weighing the arguments for and against public access, a financial disclosure system should consider its underlying objective of sharing information from disclosures.

- When sharing information with the public, a disclosure system should carefully consider the following questions: What specific information will be made available? How and where will it be accessible?

- Accessibility is a key element of public access. Countries should avoid complicated or numerous steps that can turn information that should be publicly available by law into information that, in practice, cannot be accessed.

- To increase the impact of the fight against corruption, money laundering, and financing of terrorism, as much information as possible from disclosures should be shared with other agencies.

- Sharing financial disclosure information with foreign and domestic private sector institutions can be critical to certain AML/CFT (anti-money-laundering and combating the financing of terrorism) efforts such as carrying out enhanced customer due diligence for politically exposed persons, and should thus be supported whenever possible.

Notes

1. For further information on this debate, please see StAR (2012), from page 83 onward.
2. Estimated percentages based on the 52 countries in the sample that provided information on this matter.
3. For more details on this approach, please see StAR (2012), 90.
4. Please note that this section addresses only sharing information from disclosures with other institutions. For information exchange (including the disclosure agency's receiving information from other sources), please see chapter 5 of this Guide.
5. For more on this, please see Rossi and others (2012).
6. Approximate percentage based on the 52 countries that provided information on this matter in Sample 2.
7. Approximate percentage based on the 50 countries that provided information on this matter in Sample 2.
8. This is the definition of PEPs applied in Rossi and others (2012); the same definition was first elaborated in Greenberg and others (2010).
9. See Greenberg and others (2010), 3.
10. See FATF Recommendations, specifically Recommendation 12.
11. See FATF Recommendation 22 as it applies to designated nonfinancial businesses and professions.
12. A recent revision of the FATF Recommendations clarified that enhanced due diligence should be applied not only to foreign PEPs but also to domestic PEPs. Please see FATF Recommendations 10, 12, and 22.
13. That is, these connections went undetected except by Greenberg and others (2010), StAR (2012), and Rossi and others (2012).
14. For more on this, please see https://star.worldbank.org/star/publication/public-wrongs-private-actions.

References

Djankov, S., R. La Porta, F. Lopez-de-Silanes, and A. Shleifer. 2009. "Disclosure by Politicians." Working Paper 14703, National Bureau of Economic Research, Cambridge, MA, February.

Greenberg, T., L. Gray, D. Schantz, M. Latham, and C. Garder. 2010. "Politically Exposed Persons: A Policy Paper on Strengthening Preventive Measures for the Banking Sector." World Bank, Washington, DC.

Rossi, I., L. Pop, F. Clementucci, and L. Sawaqed. 2012. "Using Asset Disclosure for Identifying Politically Exposed Persons." World Bank, Washington, DC.

StAR (Stolen Asset Recovery Initiative). 2012. *Public Office, Private Interests: Accountability through Income and Asset Disclosure*. Washington, DC: World Bank.

7. How Are Disclosures Used for Enforcement?

This chapter looks into enforcement from two perspectives. The first refers to the enforcement needed to ensure that financial disclosure systems work seamlessly. This includes everything from ensuring compliance with the requirement to declare on time and in the appropriate form to ensuring that the information submitted is accurate, as well as the different consequences—sanctions—associated with failure or irregularities in these instances. The second focuses on the use of disclosures for broader criminal investigations—for example, of corruption and money laundering.

Sanctions are the final tool by which a financial disclosure system can accomplish its objectives, as well as the final test of its effectiveness. Thus, it is important for countries to develop sanctions that are targeted, proportionate, and enforced consistently. Although this seems rather straightforward, the implementation and enforcement of sanctions have been, and still are, challenges for many countries.

The design of any sanction regime should be tailored not only to achieving the overall objectives of a financial disclosure system, but also to addressing the specific challenges within the current political and economic contexts of the country. For instance, when first introducing or implementing the system, the focus may need to be on ensuring that all required individuals submit complete disclosures on time, thus limiting sanctions to submission compliance failures. The system can then (a) expand its focus to ensuring the accuracy and veracity of disclosures and (b) expand sanctions to include other actionable offenses, such as false disclosures.

Indeed, there is a wide variation of practice in different contexts. For instance, the failure to disclose is considered a criminal offense in some countries, but not in others. Criminal sanctions may also be applied to false filing, a breach that may be easier to prove and to prosecute than would be the underlying act of corruption that the omission may have sought to conceal. See figure 7.1 for a global snapshot of sanctions.

Sanctions associated with the smooth functioning of the system are a fundamental aspect, as they are strongly linked to its overall effectiveness, reinforcing both the use of the system and the attainment of its objectives. However, these sanctions are only one side of the equation, as disclosures can also play a different role in broader investigations.

Disclosures can become a piece of a larger puzzle. In some cases, they can be the tip of the iceberg, as when the information submitted in or omitted from a disclosure

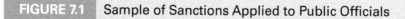

FIGURE 7.1 Sample of Sanctions Applied to Public Officials

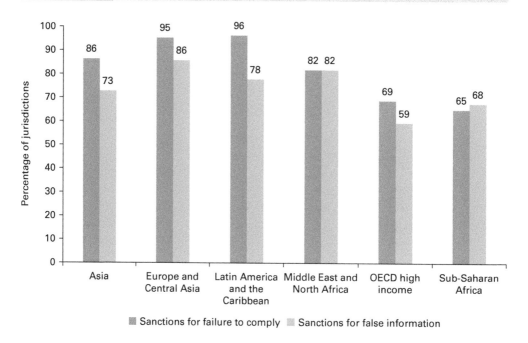

■ Sanctions for failure to comply ▦ Sanctions for false information

Note: OECD = Organisation for Economic Co-operation and Development. Approximate percentages based on the analysis of 153 jurisdictions.

provides the grounds for triggering an investigation. In other cases, they can be used as a piece of evidence in an ongoing case.

When discussing disclosure system sanctions or the use of disclosures in broader investigations, it is important to keep in mind that both aspects affect the overall strength and credibility of the system. Most public officials may not need the potential of a set of sanctions in order to submit a faithful disclosure. However, knowing that there are true consequences to misconduct and seeing that the information declared can have an impact beyond the disclosure agency can be a game changer. It can increase the deterrence effect of the system and can become an extra obstacle to consider for those involved in dishonest practices.

Section 1: Enforcement of the Disclosure System

Connecting the Dots

As discussed in previous chapters, financial disclosure regimes consist of many elements, from drafting the form to submission compliance and verification. In order for sanctions to be effective, each of these elements needs not only to work well individually, but also to connect to the next. Sanctions require "connecting the dots."

Take, for example, a situation in which resources are focused on verification but in which ensuring submission compliance is practically overlooked. In this scenario, sanctions not only will be perceived as selective enforcement, but also will punish those individuals who are attempting to comply with the requirements. Indeed, in this situation, those filing are the only ones who may be sanctioned for incomplete, late, or false filing; those who either choose not to file or neglect to file escape any punishment.

As another example, failures in the design of the form—by not clearly outlining what and how to declare—ultimately affect the final step of the system. For example, a form in one country requires that individuals declare their houses and any land they may own. What the form does not specify is that the land on which the house is built must be declared separately as land owned. Some filers do not understand this requirement and, as a result, file incorrectly. Sanctioning such officials for incomplete or false filing might be perceived as unjust in such cases of unclear instructions. Moreover, valuable resources that could have been used to follow up on violations that carry a higher corruption risk are instead used for low-risk violations.

Given that sanctions are indeed the last link in the chain, implementation data are limited, as most financial disclosure systems are still rather young and have yet to reach the stage of applying sanctions. We have also seen that countries are often unwilling or hesitant to apply sanctions of all kinds. This is largely because many disclosure systems have yet to connect all the dots in a way that would make sanctions appropriate, consistent, and just.

What Should Be Sanctionable?

Sanctionable offenses generally fall into two categories: those associated with compliance with the requirement to declare and those associated with the accuracy of submissions. This section touches on sanctions for unjustified variations of wealth. Generally, sanctions for other corrupt behavior, such as illicit enrichment and money laundering, usually fall beyond the scope of the financial disclosure regime. Sanctions for such offenses are addressed in the second section of this chapter.

Noncompliance

This broad category of sanctions deals with compliance with the requirement to declare, including failure to file, failure to file in a timely manner, and incomplete filing. These, from our experience, are the most oft-enforced sanctions and usually involve administrative penalties and/or fines (see figure 7.2).

Sanctions can be applied to multiple actors at this point in the financial disclosure process. Obviously, the filer may be sanctioned for noncompliance, but so too may the office or officer in charge of ensuring compliance. Such sanctions are intended to protect the overall functioning of the financial disclosure system and can be quite effective in doing so.

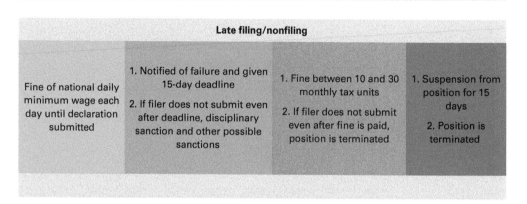

FIGURE 7.2 Sample Sanctions for Noncompliance

Late filing/nonfiling			
Fine of national daily minimum wage each day until declaration submitted	1. Notified of failure and given 15-day deadline 2. If filer does not submit even after deadline, disciplinary sanction and other possible sanctions	1. Fine between 10 and 30 monthly tax units 2. If filer does not submit even after fine is paid, position is terminated	1. Suspension from position for 15 days 2. Position is terminated

False Statement

Most financial disclosure systems outline sanctions for false statements on disclosure forms, but very few actually charge officials with this offense. Practitioners point to the fact that false statement sanctions often require *mens rea,* or an element of intent, and this requirement can be the biggest hurdle to overcome in applying this particular sanction. Omissions, often included in this category, thus pose an added challenge, as proving intent to omit information is quite difficult.

Unjustified Variations in Wealth

Because of the difficulty of catching and prosecuting corruption offenses, many jurisdictions choose to implement a system that focuses on detecting illicit enrichment by monitoring and flagging significant changes in a public official's wealth that cannot be explained by legitimate income. When discrepancies are detected between an official's disclosure and his or her legitimate income, the disclosure framework imposes sanctions for the filing of false information. In addition, however, the underlying offense concealed by the lie may also result in a separate criminal prosecution. In such cases, both the filing violation and the filer's disclosure form may be used as cause for an investigation, as assistance in an investigation, or as evidence in a prosecution.

Systems that have specific sanctions for unjustified variation of wealth in the disclosure mechanism are very rare. In one example, any variation between assets and income above a certain threshold that cannot be justified can lead to the confiscation of the asset or its equivalent value. The path to confiscation has four steps: (a) the disclosure agency files a report documenting the unjustified variation of wealth; (b) the elements of the report are reviewed by a commission of two judges and a prosecutor, which can request further information and experts' assessments, and can subpoena witnesses; (c) the commission decides whether to close the case or send it to court for a confiscation judgment; and (d) the court decides the form of confiscation (either confiscation of the assets that cannot be justified or payment of a sum of money equal to the value of the assets or expenses that cannot be justified). Within this system, courts have ordered the confiscation of about €2.8 million.[1]

Conflicts of Interest

Although many systems are designed to detect and prevent conflicts of interest, sanctions for those conflicts pose a particular problem. In many cases, the objective to sanction conflicts of interest, as well as incompatibilities, is established without ensuring sufficient education, training, and communication with filers. This ultimately serves to undermine the system rather than to bolster it.

Filers often do not know what constitutes a conflict, or even that they are at risk of one, and may learn that this is the case only once a sanction is administered. Thus, individuals may be sanctioned for unintentional violations. The culture of a system that focuses on conflicts of interest should be different than a system designed to catch unjustified variations of wealth, and, so too should the sanctions applied for such violations.

More emphasis should be placed on identifying and preventing potential conflicts of interest through a collaborative approach between the administering agency and the filer. Opportunities for dialogue, training, and guidance are key. Although severe or criminal sanctions may still be appropriate, the approach to reviewing irregularities should not impede open communication. For example, some of the most effective conflict of interest systems commit a great amount of resources to training and informing filers, all in order to prevent conflicts. Criminal sanctions may still be applied if a conflict of interest is discovered, but, for the well-informed filer, such sanctions should no longer come as a surprise.

What Types of Sanctions Should Be Available?

A range of proportional and enforceable sanctions may be applied in a disclosure system to enhance its dissuasive effect. The range of appropriate sanctions depends on the underlying objective of the system or, in other words, what the disclosure is seeking to detect and prevent. A system designed to detect and prevent illicit enrichment can function on the basis of criminal sanctions (for example, for lying on the form) and strict administrative sanctions (for example, for filing late or not filing) to ensure truthful and on-time disclosures, whereas a system focused on identifying and preventing potential conflicts of interest relies on a more collaborative approach between the administering agency and the declarant. Where severe or criminal sanctions for false statements are still applicable, they should not impede open communication and cooperation.[2]

Sanctions may range from fines to administrative sanctions (such as reprimand, demotion, suspension from office, or dismissal) and criminal penalties. The key question to consider when determining which sanctions should be used in a particular financial disclosure system is how effectively the sanctions can and will be enforced. Also, it is important to consider the complementarity between administrative and criminal sanctions, as both can be useful in different scenarios, and one can also take a gradual approach. For example, administrative procedures can be less lengthy and could produce dissuasive

FIGURE 7.3 Components of Effective Sanctions

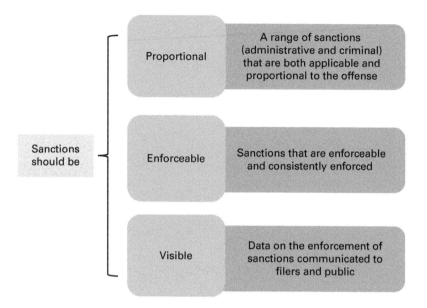

effects more quickly than could criminal sanctions. Indeed, timely and consistent response to filing failures can be more important than the severity of a sanction.

See figure 7.3 for a graphical representation of sanctions and their necessary components.

Sanctions Should Be Proportional

Fines and administrative sanctions are increasingly being used in cases of nonfiling and of late filing. This inclination toward administrative sanctions may be because such sanctions hold the greatest promise of ensuring compliance for multiple reasons, including anecdotal evidence suggesting that criminal sanctions are more difficult to enforce and are therefore rarely applied in practice.

Administrative sanctions often also carry a personal reputational or political cost that can be an effective means of compelling compliance. For instance, sanctions could include publishing the names of noncompliant officials (which could be done whether or not the content of disclosures are made

> Different categories of officials might require the use of different sanctions.

public) or linking compliance to individual performance assessments. However, the effectiveness of administrative sanctions is heavily reliant on the cultural context. In some countries, the mere threat of tarnishing one's reputation may be deterrent enough, yet in others it may have little or no effect.

More serious administrative sanctions, such as suspension or dismissal, may also be appropriate—usually for more egregious failures, such as the failure to file. That said, different categories of officials might require the use of different administrative sanctions.

In addition to administrative sanctions, some financial disclosure systems may impose criminal sanctions for serious offenses. In some countries, lying on an official document constitutes a criminal offense. This element of a financial disclosure system—that is, the potential for prosecuting someone for intentionally lying on a disclosure form—can be particularly important in the general fight against corruption. If underlying acts of corruption are suspected and, as is often the case, are difficult to prove, a specific criminal sanction for false statements can be the missing link between the official and the corrupt act.

Sanctions Should Be Enforceable

Sanctions for noncompliance with financial disclosure laws may improve compliance rates, support the credibility of the system, and signal the government's commitment to the principles that the financial disclosure system seeks to instill and enforce. However, in order to achieve these results, sanctions must be enforceable. Even well-considered, proportional, and meaningful sanctions have limited value if they are never enforced. Therefore, when determining the severity of the sanction, one must find the balance between its enforceability and its potential for deterring noncompliance. In other words, a prison term could be as ineffective as a small fine, if it is unlikely to be enforced.

As discussed earlier, sanctions can be criminal or administrative in nature, and depending on the seriousness of the breach, the latter can range from a warning and public reprimand to fines, suspension, and removal from office. One example demonstrates the challenge of finding the appropriate balance. In this case, the original penalty for filing failures was automatic termination, but it was nullified by the constitutional court for being too harsh. However, this left no form of punishment for violations. The law has since been updated to establish sanctions of salary withholding up to a certain amount and is now being enforced.

Another example demonstrates the challenges posed by a system in which unrealistically onerous fines become unenforceable in practice. What resulted was a system in which the head of the financial disclosure unit, using a matrix tied to income levels, exercised

> Authority to sanction should be clearly outlined in the legislation.

discretion to ensure that fines were reasonable and enforceable. Even with this added discretion, most of the fines are challenged, and many are eventually reduced, and, on rare occasions, eliminated. This particular example highlights yet another enforceability question: Who has the authority to sanction? Authority to sanction should be clearly identified in the legislation, but this is not always the case. Legislative challenges are discussed later in this chapter, but it is worth noting here that establishing authority and minimizing, if not eliminating, discretion is an important element in creating enforceable sanctions.

Many systems apply sanctions incrementally, so that the initial offense warrants a minimal sanction, and repeated offenses see a steady increase in the severity of sanctions. This incremental approach may help facilitate enforceability, particularly in newer systems where filers are still learning how and what to disclose. Allowing for lesser sanctions for minor or first-time offenses might also ease some of the reluctance to sanction, as filers who might receive harsher sanctions will have already been warned or lightly sanctioned and have still chosen to violate the filing requirements.

Sanctions Should Be Visible

The third essential element of effective financial disclosure sanctions is visibility. This refers to the clarity of the laws and procedures. Filers need to be aware of their obligations and of the consequences of any failures to meet said obligations. Equally important is communication of the enforcement data to the public, to provide further accountability of the system as a whole.

Frequently, when confronted with the notion of filing disclosure forms, officials' initial reactions are negative. They often view the process as cumbersome, unnecessary, and even invasive. Clearly communicating to officials not only the purpose and benefits of financial disclosure but also the filing procedure and applicable sanctions is therefore vital to compliance and to the process as a whole. Providing a visible process with clear instructions as to when, where, and how to disclose thus both creates a more functional system and ensures a more justified implementation of applicable sanctions.

The purpose and process of the system must be communicated not only to filers, but also to those who administer the process and to the general population. Communicating the compliance and enforcement data to the public speaks to the transparency, the consistency, and ultimately the credibility of the disclosure system. The release of data on submission compliance, audits, and investigations can generate support for the financial disclosure system and even enhance the credibility of an already established framework. Revealing data that show consistent treatment of filers demonstrates that the disclosure system is being administered fairly and is not a tool for political bias or manipulation.

This visibility may also support the financial disclosure agency when it comes to administering and enforcing sanctions, as in many systems these tasks may not rest with the agency. In fact, providing data on the number of cases handed over to the prosecutor's office may help apply the pressure needed to get the sanctions enforced. Some financial disclosure agencies' websites provide great examples of such visibility by listing all cases related to financial disclosure and where they are in the process.[3]

> If filers do not receive sufficiently clear and objective instructions that are backed by meaningful sanctions, they may be tempted to circumvent the disclosure system.

Regardless of the emphasis of the enforcement and sanction regime, the disclosure agency's ability to effectively define, communicate, and administer financial disclosure requirements is the cornerstone of any successful disclosure system. Without it, submission compliance is likely to be unbalanced, the system may fail to act as a deterrent of illegal activity, and the process becomes an empty bureaucratic exercise. In addition, if filers do not receive sufficiently clear and objective instructions backed by meaningful sanctions, they may be tempted to circumvent the system, either for malicious reasons or simply to avoid the nuisance of filing.

Who Is Sanctioned?

There are multiple actors in any given financial disclosure system, and failures at any level can hamper the effectiveness and credibility of the entire system. Financial disclosure systems, therefore, may provide sanctions for some or all of the actors within a given system.

All systems include some form of sanction for filers, as discussed at length earlier. However, some also include sanctions for the decentralized units in charge of collecting forms or administering sanctions. In one country, for example, a fine of one month of the national daily minimum wage is applied to disclosure administrators who do not perform their roles and responsibilities without reasonable justification. In another, a disciplinary sanction is applied for failure of the head of the division or the public officer in charge of managing disclosures to ensure that disclosures are accurate or to report omissions.

The financial disclosure agency, or the officials working within the agency, could also be sanctioned for not performing their duties. These types of sanctions often occur in systems with proactive requirements, such as the requirement to publish data, or when there is a vital breach in the process, such as leaking confidential information.

Cooperation and Coordination

As in all the other aspects of the financial disclosure system, cooperation and coordination between financial disclosure agencies, law enforcement agencies, and anticorruption bodies are key to the successful and effective implementation of sanctions.

In many countries, the agency in charge of implementing the disclosure system is separate from the enforcing agency and is therefore not ultimately responsible for ensuring successful enforcement or eventual prosecutions. In such cases, the disclosure agency is usually charged with reporting criminal violations to the prosecutor's office or other law enforcement agency for further action. Such investigations become part of the official record and can lead to or support successive investigations, often on a much larger scale. The effectiveness of the financial disclosure regime, therefore, depends on interagency collaboration. True collaboration can take time to establish, is often politicized, and depends on political will and a general culture of acceptance within the government of the importance of an effective financial disclosure system.

Cooperation and coordination, if done effectively, may also serve as a useful feedback loop to highlight any deficiencies in the financial disclosure system as a whole. If a case is forwarded to the prosecutor's office that it cannot pursue, the office can use that opportunity to explain to the financial disclosure agency what is missing. This feedback loop helps the financial disclosure system to connect the dots by highlighting failures that hinder enforcement. Whether the failures are deficiencies in the form, in verification, or even in the legislation, this feedback can only help to strengthen a financial disclosure system.

Take, for example, a situation in which it becomes clear to the financial disclosure agency that the prosecutor's office is not actively pursuing any of the cases forwarded from the agency. This feedback may inform the agency and legislators that more or harsher administrative sanctions need to be available and applied, thereby reducing reliance on the justice system to enforce the disclosure requirement.

Challenges in Imposing Sanctions

As explained earlier, enforcing sanctions for noncompliance requires proportionality, enforcement, and visibility. The implementation of these three key elements of an effective financial disclosure regime raises many significant challenges. This subsection addresses a few that merit further discussion.

Poorly Drafted Legislation

Legislation establishing the financial disclosure agency and disclosure requirements is central to any financial disclosure system. Ensuring that this legislation is thorough, clear, consistent, and enforceable is a step that is often overlooked in the drafting process. Thus, in many situations, important questions are left unanswered, only to cause confusion in the implementation of the law and, as an extension, in the sanctioning of infractions.

Some examples of such challenges include one system in which the law does not provide clear guidance about the exact form or magnitude of sanctions that can and should be applied for filing failures. In another country, the law and corresponding sanction set forth by the financial disclosure system are inconsistent with existing criminal laws and, as such, can not be enforced.

Another issue in the drafting of financial disclosure legislation is the establishment of requirements that may hinder the ability to sanction filers. For example, in one country, the system presents the possibility of very serious consequences for officials convicted of corrupt acts. However, there is evidence that such tough sanctions may also undermine enforcement of financial disclosure requirements by making the agency staff members reluctant to charge officials who have been accused of failing to fill out their financial disclosure forms completely or correctly. In addition, the legislation requires "proof of malicious intent," which is usually difficult to produce. Perhaps if the law contemplated a range of administrative sanctions for noncompliance, it is conceivable that it could have resulted in a greater number of successfully enforced sanctions.

The Political Nature of Sanctions

Another challenge for national authorities is developing the institutional capacity to assert independence and to be vigilant against potential abuse of sanctioning powers. In many countries, this may require investing in building the capacity of prosecutors, the judiciary, and law enforcement while ensuring their independence and impartiality.

Though there is limited evidence that sanctions are actually applied for malicious reasons, such as to punish or tarnish the reputation of political opponents, the best defense against this particular challenge is clear legislation with transparent enforcement. If the sanctions are applied in a consistent and visible manner, it is difficult to assert any political bias. That said, consistency in enforcing sanctions is often quite difficult given the political nature of the parties involved. For instance, prosecutors in many countries actively seek to prosecute the "big fish" for the sake of publicity, often overlooking or dismissing valid yet less sensational cases.

Inadequate Rule of Law

Rule of law is integral to and indispensable for good governance, security, development, and human rights. Unfortunately, jurisdictions that have a pressing need to stamp out corruption often also have a pressing need to strengthen their rule of law. Many fear that a system based on criminal sanctions or fines may be fraught with challenges if the broader legal system cannot be relied upon to impose those sanctions. Without the ability to prosecute failures, such sanctions would become meaningless and would undermine the credibility of the system. This is a valid concern, and countries seeking to implement and enforce financial disclosure systems would be well advised to look carefully at the overall legal and judicial climate. Laws and legal procedures are indeed essential, but so are effective, transparent, and independent institutions.

> When sanctions are applied in a consistent and visible manner, it becomes increasingly difficult to assert any political bias.

Constitutional Challenges

Countries in the midst of establishing or improving their financial disclosure must often consider the constitutionality of sanctioning financial disclosure violations. For the most part, this concern is largely unfounded and most often reflects the concerns and challenges just mentioned rather than constitutional issues.

For example, the constitutional protection of the presumption of innocence places the onus on the state to prove the guilt of an accused person, thus relieving the accused of any burden to prove his or her innocence. However, this principle does not preclude legislatures from creating offenses containing a rebuttable presumption, so long as the principles of rationality and proportionality are duly respected. This reasoning can be extended to public servants, who, in assuming a position of trust, subject themselves to the legal requirements and to the administrative and criminal sanctions that arise from the abuse of that trust. In this context, providing information regarding the sources of income and assets does not appear as a significant or unfair burden for filers, and neither does sanctioning officials who fail to disclose.

Countries with the proper legal and institutional safeguards in place are able to prosecute financial disclosure offenses, thereby turning these sanctions into an effective accountability and transparency mechanism.

Section 2: Disclosures as Part of a Bigger Puzzle: How Can Disclosure Support the Broader Fight against Corruption and Asset Recovery?

The raw information in financial disclosures and the analytical findings coming out of the verification process are resources that have been underutilized in the fight against corruption and money laundering, and in efforts to recover assets.

The term *raw data* refers to information declared by a filer before any analysis by the disclosure agency. *Results of the analysis* or *verification of financial disclosures* carried out by a disclosure agency can point to a discrepancy, inconsistency, or red flag. For example, in the course of the verification process, the financial disclosure agency might find a significant increase in the income declared by an official between two years, a change in assets that does not match the sources of income declared, or very high sums of money received as loans from individuals. Depending on the mandate and resources of the agency, the information that would be included in notifications to other entities can range from a simple inconsistency to the results of a comprehensive analysis (that can include even the receipt of information from financial institutions).

Both the raw data and the results of the analysis of financial disclosures can be useful in the analysis of suspicious transaction reports by financial intelligence units (FIUs) and can positively affect the quality of the intelligence that reaches investigators and prosecutors who are working on corruption and money-laundering cases.

In 2012, the World Bank carried out a survey on the use of financial disclosures among FIUs in the Sub-Saharan Africa, Europe and Central Asia, East Asia and Pacific, and Middle East and North Africa regions. Of 30 FIUs from countries with functioning disclosure systems, 16 responded that they used financial disclosures for the analysis of suspicious transaction reports about public officials or politically exposed persons (PEPs). This shows that there is a growing understanding among FIUs of the usefulness of financial disclosures in their operations. However, there is also ample room for growth.

Beyond FIUs, the information in financial disclosures or the results of the verification of financial disclosures can both trigger corruption or money-laundering investigations and become a piece of evidence in a case. Not only may this evidence be useful in countries where illicit enrichment is criminalized, but also the entries made in disclosures may provide circumstantial evidence that supports action in broader investigations. For example, in one investigation, it was challenging to establish the link between a public official and an overseas company through which bribe payments were made, mainly because of legal provisions in the jurisdiction where the company was founded. However, once the investigators accessed the financial disclosure of the official, they could see that he had declared his interest in the overseas company. In this situation, the financial disclosure helped the investigators both overcome a substantial challenge and shorten one phase of the investigation.

In some jurisdictions, financial disclosure agencies are specifically mandated in the legislation to notify tax authorities when they find indications of potential tax code violations. Even if this is not specified in the legislation, when an agency is looking to investigate potential illicit assets, it should consider a method that is often referred to as the "Al Capone" approach.[4] Where the verification process has identified assets that are not commensurate with lawful income, then involving the tax authorities with a view to identifying and invoking penalties for failing to declare income is an approach that directly attacks the asset base of the filer. The linkage with the work of tax authorities is, in some countries, further strengthened by the fact that the financial disclosure system is managed by the tax administration.

Illicit Enrichment

The offense of illicit enrichment was designed and included in the United Nations Convention Against Corruption (UNCAC) as a measure to combat corruption by facilitating the usually challenging act of demonstrating that the unexplained wealth of an individual is the result of criminal activity.[5] Under more conventional approaches to prosecuting corruption, this link would normally have to be proven by the prosecution. The criminalization of illicit enrichment allows instead for a *prima facie* case to be established by determining that an individual's wealth is disproportionate to his or her legitimate sources of income and by reversing the burden of proof to that individual.

In some countries, illicit enrichment is classified as a criminal offense, and the system is equipped to detect discrepancies between an official's disclosures and other sources of information about his or her income and assets. These countries have an additional method for attacking the wealth of corrupt public officials. An investigation into illicit enrichment may also serve as a trigger for a broader investigation to establish both the underlying criminal activities and the identity of other parties possibly involved in the corruption.

Asset Recovery

Financial disclosures can provide useful circumstantial evidence to support international cooperation in recovering assets.[6] The disclosure can strengthen the request for information through FIU or police channels (informal assistance) or mutual legal assistance channels (formal assistance). For example, the information in financial disclosures or the results of the verification process can support the link between the filer and the jurisdiction that receives the request for mutual legal assistance.

The content and verification of a financial disclosure can also be helpful in the context of a money-laundering investigation carried out by the foreign jurisdiction in which the assets of the public official of another country are held. Consider the following example: if during the period for which an official files a disclosure, he or she accumulated assets abroad well in excess of his or her declared income, then the disclosure—though not proving criminal conduct—could be circumstantial evidence that supports the inference that the property in question has criminal origins. In such a case, the information in the financial disclosure could support the restraint and ultimate confiscation of those assets.

An example worthy of mention and a situation in which a presumption about the illicit origin of assets provides for their freezing, forfeiture, or restitution is detailed in Switzerland's administrative confiscation provisions, specifically those that relate to assets held by foreign PEPs and their associates in Switzerland. The Swiss Federal Administrative Court can assume that assets have an illicit origin when "the wealth of the person who holds powers of disposal over the assets has been subject to an extraordinary increase that is connected with the exercise of a public office by the politically exposed person and the level of corruption in the country of origin or surrounding the politically exposed person in question during his or her term of office was acknowledged as high" (Federal Council 2015, art. 6). This presumption can be rejected by the court if it can be demonstrated that, in all probability, the assets were acquired by lawful means; however, from an investigative perspective, any financial disclosures of the PEP could provide useful circumstantial evidence to either support or negate the illicit origin.

Chapter 7—Key Recommendations

- Enforcement is the *final step* available for a financial disclosure system to accomplish its objectives: knowing that there are true consequences for misconduct can increase the deterrence effect of system. Thus, there should be sanctions for all forms of misconduct, including noncompliance, false statements, unjustified variations of wealth, and conflicts of interest.

- In order to be effective and fair, sanctions must be *targeted* and *enforced consistently.*

- Sanctions should be the following:
  - *Linked to the objective of the system.* Illicit enrichment and conflict of interest violations require different approaches.
  - *Proportional.* Applying less severe sanctions for failure to file than for submission of inaccurate information may be more beneficial to the effectiveness of the system.
  - *Enforceable.* Sanctions must be balanced. Authority to sanction should be clearly outlined in the legislation.

(continued next page)

- *Visible.* Filers must be aware of their obligations and the sanctions for not complying with them. Communication about enforcement data is also key.

- Countries should identify and work toward reducing barriers to the application of effective and fair sanctions, such as poorly drafted legislation, political interference with enforcement, inadequate rule of law, and constitutional challenges.

Notes

1. For detailed information on these cases, please refer to https://www.integritate.eu /HOTARARI-DEFINITIVE-SI-IREVOCABILE-ALE-INSTANTELOR-DE -JUDECATA/CONFISCĂRI-DE-AVERE.aspx and www.integritate.eu/Noutati.aspx? PID=243&M=NewsV2&Action=1&NewsId=2115.
2. An official may be reluctant to inquire about potential conflicts of interest when the same agency is also charged with investigating and prosecuting those actions. Therefore, some governments provide separate agencies or departments for guidance and for enforcement.
3. For example, in the case of Romania, see http://www.integritate.eu.
4. This term was coined from the investigation of Alphonse Gabriel "Al" Capone, a prohibition-era gang leader who engaged in a variety of criminal activities, including racketeering, bootlegging of liquor, prostitution, and bribery of government officials. He was ultimately arrested for and convicted of tax evasion, for which he served an 11-year prison sentence. This investigative approach involves multiple law enforcement agencies working in concert, targeting suspects with any viable legal processes and charges that develop.
5. For more on this, see http://www.unodc.org/documents/treaties/UNCAC/COSP /session6/V1505880e.pdf.
6. For more on this, see http://www.unodc.org/documents/treaties/UNCAC /WorkingGroups/EMInternationalCooperation/2-3November2015/V1506265e .pdf.

Appendix A. Sample 1 and Sample 2 Data

This appendix provides information on the data sets that were collected by the Financial Market Integrity team of the World Bank Group. The data covered in Sample 1 (legislation) have been gathered since 2007[1] with continuous updates, the last one in 2015. The data in Sample 2 were collected only in 2015. Both samples were used for the analysis throughout this Guide. [2]

Sample 1: Legislation

This sample consists of 176 countries, of which 161 have a disclosure system.[3] Although disclosure requirements can apply to different categories of public officials, we have focused our legal analysis on disclosure requirements for members of the legislative and executive branches. The disclosure requirements in those 161 countries[4] are applicable to members of the legislative branch in only 10 countries, members of the executive branch in only 17 countries, and members of both branches in 134 countries. See table A.1 for a regional breakdown and table A.2 for a breakdown by income category.[5]

TABLE A.1	Sample 1 Countries, by Region	
Region	Number of countries	Countries and economies in the subsample
OECD high income (OECD)	32	Australia; Austria; Belgium; Canada; Chile; Czech Republic; Denmark; Estonia; Finland; France; Germany; Greece; Hungary; Iceland; Ireland; Israel; Italy; Japan; Korea, Rep.; Luxembourg; Netherlands; New Zealand; Norway; Poland; Portugal; Slovak Republic; Slovenia; Spain; Sweden; Switzerland; United Kingdom; United States
Sub-Saharan Africa (SSA)	45	Angola; Benin; Botswana; Burkina Faso; Burundi; Cabo Verde; Cameroon; Central African Republic; Chad; Comoros; Congo, Dem. Rep.; Congo, Rep.; Côte d'Ivoire; Eritrea; Ethiopia; Gabon; Gambia, The; Ghana; Guinea; Guinea-Bissau; Kenya; Lesotho; Liberia; Madagascar; Malawi; Mali; Mauritania; Mauritius; Mozambique; Namibia; Niger; Nigeria; Rwanda; São Tomé and Príncipe; Senegal; Seychelles; Sierra Leone; South Africa; Sudan; Swaziland; Tanzania; Togo; Uganda; Zambia; Zimbabwe

(continued next page)

TABLE A.1	Sample 1 Countries, by Region *(continued)*	
Region	Number of countries	Countries and economies in the subsample
Asia	30	Afghanistan; Bangladesh; Bhutan; Brunei Darussalam; Cambodia; China; Fiji; Hong Kong SAR, China; India; Indonesia; Kiribati; Lao PDR; Malaysia; Maldives; Micronesia, Fed. Sts.; Mongolia; Palau; Papua New Guinea; Pakistan; Philippines; Samoa; Singapore; Solomon Islands; Sri Lanka; Taiwan, China; Thailand; Timor-Leste; Tonga; Vanuatu; Vietnam
Europe and Central Asia (ECA)	22	Albania; Armenia; Azerbaijan; Belarus; Bosnia and Herzegovina; Bulgaria; Croatia; Georgia; Kazakhstan; Kyrgyz Republic; Latvia; Lithuania; Macedonia, FYR; Moldova; Montenegro; Romania; Russian Federation; Serbia; Tajikistan; Turkey; Ukraine; Uzbekistan
Latin America and the Caribbean (LAC)	29	Antigua and Barbuda; Argentina; Bahamas, The; Belize; Bolivia; Brazil; Colombia; Costa Rica; Dominica; Dominican Republic; Ecuador; El Salvador; Guatemala; Guyana; Haiti; Honduras; Jamaica; Mexico; Nicaragua; Panama; Paraguay; Peru; Puerto Rico; St. Lucia; St. Vincent and the Grenadines; Suriname; Trinidad and Tobago; Uruguay; Venezuela, RB
Middle East and North Africa (MENA)	18	Algeria; Bahrain; Djibouti; Egypt, Arab Rep.; Iran, Islamic Rep.; Iraq; Jordan; Kuwait; Lebanon; Morocco; Oman; Qatar; Saudi Arabia; Syrian Arab Republic; Tunisia; United Arab Emirates; West Bank and Gaza; Yemen, Rep.

Note: OECD = Organisation for Economic Co-operation and Development.

TABLE A.2	Sample 1 Countries, by Income Category	
Income category	Number of countries	Countries and economies in the subsample
High income	54	Antigua and Barbuda; Argentina; Australia; Austria; Bahamas, The; Bahrain; Belgium; Brunei Darussalam; Canada; Chile; Croatia; Czech Republic; Denmark; Estonia; Finland; France; Germany; Greece; Hong Kong SAR, China; Hungary; Iceland; Ireland; Israel; Italy; Japan; Korea, Rep.; Kuwait; Latvia; Lithuania; Luxembourg; Netherlands; New Zealand; Norway; Oman; Poland; Portugal; Puerto Rico; Qatar; Russian Federation; Saudi Arabia; Seychelles; Singapore; Slovak Republic; Slovenia; Spain; Sweden; Switzerland; Taiwan, China; Trinidad and Tobago; United Arab Emirates; United Kingdom; United States; Uruguay; Venezuela, RB

(continued next page)

TABLE A.2	Sample 1 Countries, by Income Category *(continued)*	
Income category	Number of countries	Countries and economies in the subsample
Upper-middle income	46	Albania; Algeria; Angola; Azerbaijan; Belarus; Belize; Bosnia and Herzegovina; Botswana; Brazil; Bulgaria; China; Colombia; Costa Rica; Dominica; Dominican Republic; Ecuador; Fiji; Gabon; Iran, Islamic Rep.; Iraq; Jamaica; Jordan; Kazakhstan; Lebanon; Macedonia, FYR; Malaysia; Maldives; Mauritius; Mexico; Mongolia; Montenegro; Namibia; Palau; Panama; Paraguay; Peru; Romania; Serbia; South Africa; St. Lucia; St. Vincent and the Grenadines; Suriname; Thailand; Tonga; Tunisia; Turkey
Lower-middle income	49	Armenia; Bangladesh; Bhutan; Bolivia; Cabo Verde; Cameroon; Congo, Rep.; Côte d'Ivoire; Djibouti; Egypt, Arab Rep.; El Salvador; Georgia; Ghana; Guatemala; Guyana; Honduras; India; Indonesia; Kenya; Kiribati; Kyrgyz Republic; Lao PDR; Lesotho; Mauritania; Micronesia, Fed. Sts.; Moldova; Morocco; Nicaragua; Nigeria; Pakistan; Papua New Guinea; Philippines; Samoa; São Tomé and Príncipe; Senegal; Solomon Islands; Sri Lanka; Sudan; Swaziland; Syrian Arab Republic; Tajikistan; Timor-Leste; Ukraine; Uzbekistan; Vanuatu; Vietnam; West Bank and Gaza; Yemen, Rep.; Zambia
Low income	27	Afghanistan; Benin; Burkina Faso; Burundi; Cambodia; Central African Republic; Chad; Comoros; Congo, Dem. Rep.; Eritrea; Ethiopia; Gambia, The; Guinea; Guinea-Bissau; Haiti; Liberia; Madagascar; Malawi; Mali; Mozambique; Niger; Rwanda; Sierra Leone; Tanzania; Togo; Uganda; Zimbabwe

Source: World Bank FY15 country and lending groups, available at http://data.worldbank.org/about/country-and-lending-groups.

Sample 2: Practices of Disclosure Agencies

The sample consists of 52 countries. The regional breakdown appears in table A.3, and the breakdown by income category in table A.4.[6]

TABLE A.3	Sample 2 Countries, by Region	
Region	Number of countries	Countries and economies in the subsample
OECD high income (OECD)	8	Belgium; Canada; Chile; France; Israel; Japan; Korea, Rep.; United States
Sub-Saharan Africa (SSA)	11	Burkina Faso; Ethiopia; Gabon; Kenya; Mauritius; Nigeria; Rwanda; Seychelles; South Africa; Tanzania; Uganda
Asia	9	Bhutan; China; Indonesia; Malaysia; Mongolia; Philippines; Sri Lanka; Thailand; Vietnam
Europe and Central Asia (ECA)	10	Albania; Armenia; Georgia; Kazakhstan; Latvia; Lithuania; Macedonia, FYR; Moldova; Romania; Serbia
Latin America and the Caribbean (LAC)	11	Argentina; Bolivia; Brazil; Colombia; Costa Rica; Dominican Republic; El Salvador; Honduras; Jamaica; Peru; Trinidad and Tobago
Middle East and North Africa (MENA)	3	Egypt, Arab Rep.; Iraq; Morocco

Note: OECD = Organisation for Economic Co-operation and Development.

TABLE A.4	Sample 2 Countries, by Income Category	
Income category	Number of countries	Countries and economies in the subsample
High-income	13	Argentina; Belgium; Canada; Chile; France; Israel; Japan; Korea, Rep.; Latvia; Lithuania; Seychelles; Trinidad and Tobago; United States
Upper-middle income	19	Albania; Brazil; China; Colombia; Costa Rica; Dominican Republic; Gabon; Iraq; Jamaica; Kazakhstan; Macedonia, FYR; Malaysia; Mauritius; Mongolia; Peru; Romania; Serbia; South Africa; Thailand
Lower-middle income	15	Armenia; Bhutan; Bolivia; Egypt, Arab Rep.; El Salvador; Georgia; Honduras; Indonesia; Kenya; Moldova; Morocco; Nigeria; Philippines; Sri Lanka; Vietnam
Low-income	5	Burkina Faso; Ethiopia; Rwanda; Tanzania; Uganda

Source: World Bank FY15 country and lending groups, available at http://data.worldbank.org/about/country-and-lending-groups.

Notes

1. A previous version of this data set was used in the paper by Djankov and others (2009).
2. The sample used for each figure appears in the figure's notes. Please note that, in some figures, a country may have not provided information in the survey used to collect the data in the sample, or their experience may not be relevant for the analysis. For example, a country that does not perform verification would not be part of the sample in the figure analyzing verification processes.
3. In our sample, 15 countries do not have a disclosure system. These are Botswana, Brunei Darussalam, Eritrea, Kiribati, the Federated States of Micronesia, Oman, Qatar, Samoa, Saudi Arabia, St. Vincent and the Grenadines, Suriname, the Syrian Arab Republic, Tonga, the United Arab Emirates, and Uzbekistan.
4. Please note that, of the 161 countries in our sample that have a disclosure system, we were unable to find implementation information on 8 of them. Therefore, many of the figures and graphs in this Guide were constructed from data on 153 jurisdictions.
5. Please note that we have made some minor changes to the World Bank FY15 country and lending group classification, available at http://data.worldbank.org/about/country-and-lending-groups. More specifically, two regions—South Asia, and East Asia and Pacific—have been merged into one, and two lending groups—Asia and OECD high income—have been included as one for the regional classification.
6. Please note that we have made some minor changes to the World Bank FY15 country and lending groups classification, available at http://data.worldbank.org/about/country-and-lending-groups. More specifically, two regions—South Asia, and East Asia and Pacific—have been merged into one, and Asia and OECD high income have been included as one group for the regional classification.

Reference

Djankov, S., R. La Porta, F. Lopez-de-Silanes, and A. Shleifer. 2009. "Disclosure by Politicians." Working Paper 14703, National Bureau of Economic Research, Cambridge, MA, http://www.nber.org/papers/w14703.